The Priory of Sion

Legacy of Rennes-le-chateau and the Priory of Sion

(Revelations From the World's Most Secret Society - Guardians)

Nancy Rivera

Published By **Regina Loviusher**

Nancy Rivera

The Priory of Sion: Legacy of Rennes-le-chateau and the Priory of Sion (Revelations From the World's Most Secret Society - Guardians)

ISBN   978-1-77485-669-7

No part of this guidebook shall be reproduced in any form without permission in writing from the publisher except in the case of brief quotations embodied in critical articles or reviews.

Legal & Disclaimer

The information contained in this ebook is not designed to replace or take the place of any form of medicine or professional medical advice. The information in this ebook has been provided for educational & entertainment purposes only.

The information contained in this book has been compiled from sources deemed reliable, and it is accurate to the best of the Author's knowledge; however, the Author cannot guarantee its accuracy and validity and cannot be held liable for any errors or omissions. Changes are periodically made to this book. You must consult your doctor or get professional medical advice before using any of the suggested remedies, techniques, or information in this book.

Upon using the information contained in this book, you agree to hold harmless the Author from and against any damages, costs, and expenses, including any legal fees potentially resulting from the application of any of the information provided by this guide. This disclaimer applies to any damages or injury caused by the use and application, whether directly or indirectly, of any advice or information presented, whether for breach of contract, tort, negligence, personal injury, criminal intent, or under any other cause of action.

You agree to accept all risks of using the information presented inside this book. You need to consult a professional medical practitioner in order to ensure you are both able and healthy enough to participate in this program.

TABLE OF CONTENTS

Introduction

Hoax or conspiracy or secret society? These are the kinds of reactions you can expect to get when you mention the concept that there is a secret society called The Priory of Sion. It is a shady order that was created to hide what is true about followers from Jesus Christ, the group are portrayed as an elaborate concoction or as the most effective secret society that exists. Are they genuine? What is their secret? Where are they from? What impact will they be able to have on the world? These are the kinds of questions this book aims to solve.

The underlying tale that is The Priory of Sion is the almost heretical belief the idea that Jesus Christ -- the supposed god-son of God was the father of children. It's not just that, but that his bloodline continues until the present day. If it is true, this could have a major impact on the existence of Christianity which is the most popular religion in the world. If the Priory (as is supposed to be, are protecting the truth regarding this subject, they may hold one of the more influential information available. Imagine it as an ideological bomb in motion and poised to explode into the consciousness of the entire world.

In addition, the people who are believed to guard these secrets are considered as some of the most brilliant thinkers of all time. Isaac Newton, Nicholas Flamel as well as Leonardo da Vinci have all been linked to the order although their roles are controversial. In reality, the entire existence of the Order has been debated. Some believe that, as opposed to an underground society it is a hoax. Priory is actually an elaborate fraud.

Others believe that these accusations are just a way to cover up the truth. What do we know with certainty? Who exactly is the members of the Priory of Sion?

Chapter 1: Hidden Evidence

The most significant elements of this story is the battle. One side has an American and is forced to defend himself. On the other three Englishmen are convinced that they've been robbed, and their thoughts are portrayed as absurd. It's as if their reputation has been damaged. They want to be satisfied. Every side is spending many thousands to compete against each other. The battle cannot be resolved until one side is victorious. However, unlike a medieval fighting or Victorian duel this is a modern battle. Although the background of the Priory of Sion is said to go back many thousands of years, this battle took place after the start of the millennium II. The location was at the Royal Courts of Justice in the area of London called the Strand. The year of the event is 2006.

We will begin. Nowadays, it's impossible to talk about Sion's Priory of Sion without mentioning several books. They are all popular they range from an international bestseller that made its author millionaires and a supposed academic work that defied the odds and left an impression across the globe, and lastly, an obscure French text that is widely believed to be the one that being the catalyst for this entire story. The story is well-suited to it. which may or may not be accurate, the production of books is inextricably tied in their Priory in every way. We will discover that the writing, studying, as well as the effect of these books are crucial to the narrative.

Two of these books were written by two men who fought each other on the Strand. One side there was Dan Brown, writer of The Da Vinci Code, and is often is credited with turning The Priory of Sion into a worldwide concern. He was slammed by the Catholic Church and dismissed by critics, Brown's work has nonetheless proven to be a hit beyond imagination. For the professor at the university this has been an industry that is thriving. Being a teacher of others writers and publish stories, there are very few on earth better equipped to show people how to make money from stories. The way that the story got its start is the main issue in this court battle.

On the opposite part of the courtroom, there are two males and their team of lawyers. Richard Leigh, hailing from New Jersey, and Michael Baigent and Michael Baigent, who hail from New Zealand. They are giddy at Dan Brown (who, strangely is from New Hampshire) from the opposite part of Court 61. Dan Brown is the defendant and two other men accuse that he is a plagiarism. Brown claims to have not only stole their ideas and then exposed their ideas before the public in a manner that discredited the work they'd done. Baigent Leigh and Baigent Leigh are more well-known to the world for being the authors of The Holy Blood and the Holy Grail. In addition to being among the most well-known pieces of writing ever produced in the field of The Holy Grail, their book introduces the concept that there was a Priory of Sion to an audience of English speakers. We'll see soon the work of theirs was extremely success and only a handful of writers have come close to providing as revolutionary as controversial, as controversial, and as lucrative a perspective on religion over the past three centuries.

So both courts are populated by writers. Today the verdict will be made that will give credibility to (or destroy the credibility of) an idea believed to be dated back nearly two thousand years. The core of this issue, and the judge poised to rule on the claims of the Priory of Sion. Through the work of both sides of the debate the name of the Priory has been heard by more people than anyone could have ever imagined. However, while Brown has dominated the bestseller charts across the globe in fiction Baigent as well as Leigh (as as a third writer that is not in the picture however, and is expected to be mentioned in the near future) made huge waves in the realm of non-fiction. Between them, they've been dominant on both sides of bestseller charts.

This is among the most important aspects that underlie the matter and, in turn, it is the very existence of the Priory of Sion itself. There's a great deal of profit to be made from publishing these theories. It is unclear if this is because they're dangerous due to their illuminating nature or enjoyable, is not clarified. Just because they never went to court, there's the possibility of earning money through publishing books on Sion's Priory of Sion. With the court cases that are like those, there's an enormous amount of money that could be lost.

What exactly was the pair of Baigent and Leigh saying during Courtroom 61? Their case wasn't so straightforward as a typical case of plagiarism. In most cases of plagiarism the prosecution must show that the defendant merely copied their concept and turned an income from it without crediting them or sharing the profits. This has happened countless instances in the past, and in the realm of publication (and the media as a whole) it's not uncommon. However, this particular instance was a bit different.

Particularly, Baigent and Leigh claimed that Brown In The Da Vinci Code -used the plot "directly copied" from their work, The Holy Blood and the Holy Grail. The idea was copied was, according to them, a way for Brown to earn a massive sum of money using the concepts of the authors who wrote it. When the trial it was estimated that Brown's writing was worth over $45 million. Alongside writing the novel, we also had a multi-million dollar film franchise that starred Tom Hanks. Da Vinci Code Da Vinci Code had achieved enormous success, possibly next to Harry Potter alone in terms of post-millennial success in publishing. The success, as according to the prosecution was based on the foundation of concepts that were derived in bulk directly from The Holy Blood and the Holy Grail.

This isn't to suggest it was not successful. The Holy Blood and the Holy Grail was not an incredibly successful book in its own way. It's not the case at all. In fact, when it was published during the 80s, this book created quite a stir. It was nevertheless regarded (by both the authors and the readers) as an non-fiction work. If you visit any bookshop in search of The Holy Blood and the Holy Grail and it'll be in the section of non-fiction. It was, in fact, not being in the modern age section or religious section The Holy Blood and the Holy Grail was nestled amid other more substantial books under the umbrella of the past. This was the genre that the book was a leader in. Non-fiction books generally do not sell in massive quantities, but this was unique. Perhaps due to the fact that it was able to move from the realm of speculative theology, which many people shun, to the realms of accepted historicalism It had become incredibly well-known.

This is where the issue lies. For the writers of The Holy Blood and the Holy Grail The mere existence of The Da Vinci Code undermined their work. It was not only that ideas were borrowed from the original text and presented as a fictionalized world and led to their questioning. As convinced as they were of the fact that The Priory of Sion was a actual, functioning institution and that it was a functioning institution, the manner in which Dan Brown had taken and presented his ideas was a reversal of the work they'd accomplished to this point. The future success of their films (and those in the subsequent sequels of The Holy Blood and the Holy Grail) were damaged due to the existence the existence of The Da Vinci Code. That's the reason they filed lawsuits.

At that point it seemed like money was far from the subject. Baigent, Leigh, and Henry Lincoln (the third writer) had already been wealthy men. Their research into the eventual topic of The Holy Blood and the

Holy Grail had turned them from struggling writers to experts in the field of their knowledge of the Holy Grail and, in particular specifically, the Priory of Sion. Michael Baigent was even quoted in the time of his interview as saying "Whether our hypothesis is correct or not is not important." The case was not a bid to obtain punitive damages instead, it was to defend their theories as well as to safeguard their integrity, as well as to protect the concept about Sion as the Priory of Sion. According to what Michael Baigent said, the writers were of the opinion that they were left with "no alternative."

Baigent and Leigh both resented "being included" with the work of fiction referred to in the form of The Da Vinci Code. In their constant rants that they were not, in the press it appeared more and more as if they were in fact on a high-minded effort to defend their intellectual property against the backdrop of a massive swathe of the world of fiction. It was as if they were the guardians of the authenticity of the Priory of Sion, holding their hands against the sloppy version made available before the public by insensitive Dan Brown. Like anyone within the publishing industry will inform you, a non-fiction Bestseller (such like The Holy Blood and the Holy Grail) may earn praise and admiration while a bestseller in fiction (such like The Da Vinci Code) will always earn income. Therefore, while Baigent as well as Leigh were determined to preserve their integrity as well as that the integrity of their works, Dan Brown and his publishers were determined to keep their lucrative channels open. So, the two men were in a courtroom, fighting with each other in the London courtroom.

The key to Baigent's argument (and the legal arguments of his Team) was the notion of "historical significance." The Holy Blood and the Holy Grail, the authors claimed was a scholarly historical source. It was a text they had spent hours researching and compiling. It was a work that they had spent years researching and putting together. Da Vinci Code, if was read by millions, could have ruined the supposed authenticity of the historical accuracy of the non-fiction work. It wasn't plagiarism at all however this was the argument Baigent repeatedly repeated repeatedly in the media.

The idea did go against the common logic. Perhaps, if a reader was to sit down and read either they would be able to discern that the first was a work of fiction, while the other an non-fiction piece? The tone, the presentation, design, and even the design of the cover would inform them of this. So long as The Da Vinci Code veered away from quoting the verbatim passages of the other book without acknowledging them, how would this "historical implications" influence The Holy Blood and the Holy Grail?

In addition, if the claimed story told by the writers of The Holy Blood and the Holy Grail was indeed held to be accurate The facts ought to be accessible to fiction writers regardless of whether or not they appear in a specific novel or otherwise. If writing about history, textbook writers are not likely to have their authors in court over the reference to or mentioning of the Battle of Hastings or the Spanish Inquisition. If the novel that was written by Baigent and his co-writers was founded on facts (as is the basis of fiction) then there was nothing problem in Dan Brown making use of ideas like The Priory of Sion. Priory of Sion, and the secrets they kept.

Three weeks were needed for the court to come to a conclusion. The judge who was assigned to that case Peter Smith, seemed to be enjoying his time in the spotlight. It is not often within the British legal system, it was apparent that he was allowed to participate in such a dramatic yet also so straight-forward an instance. It was not a surprise when Judge Smith ruled in the favor of the defendant, Dan Brown. The judge did not only decide in this manner however, he also was able to offer an opinion on the charges which were spewed in the courtroom by lawyers Baigent as well as Leigh. The argument, as the judge declared appeared to be "vague." It was clear that they changed their strategy throughout the trial and even based their whole argument on the "weak base."

As previously mentioned the case was a significant incident. Along with the publishing rights and profits included in the lawsuit the issue of legal fees was settled by the justices. It took Baigent and Leigh more than 1 million dollars to pursue Dan Brown. Since they were litigating in Britain and not in the United States, the cost was generally referred to as about 800,000. In reality, they did not have a hard time obtaining a verdict and lose even more money. Dan Brown's team of lawyers (and the ones from his publisher) was more costly. It was PS1.2 million. The judge had required Leigh as well as Baigent to pay for 85 percent of Brown's legal expenses the two authors were hit with a huge amount. Like most people in this case they sought an appeal. At the time the appeal was done the legal fees increased to more than PS3 million. It's only a tiny portion of the funds used in current discussions regarding The Priory of Sion, and is an illustration of the reason why this subject is so hotly debated.

The consequences of the judge's decision did not stop at claiming that one side was right and the other side was wrong. The case also included a textual analysis of both books. The case was ruled to Judge Smith, this comparison may provide understanding of the way that both books were made and the reason why the common element in both of them - that of the Priory of Sion and the concepts it claims to safeguard is an issue of controversy. The story of the way Baigent, Lincoln, and Leigh were the authors was quite distinct (a subject we'll come to in a moment) the analysis of how the concept came about was able in order to prove to the Judge that the book was not plagiarism.

As per Dan Brown and his legal defense, the story of the Priory of Sion was told to Dan Brown by his wife. Blythe Brown is considered to be an expert in the field of art and frequently sources for the books of her husband she had read The Holy Blood and the Holy Grail. As an expert in art she was acquainted with the key characters in the book. She also discovered an innovative approach to the concepts that she was so interested in that she decided to present the ideas and shared them with her husband. Blythe gave Dan with a quick overview of the concepts outlined in the book. These ideas that would eventually come together to form The Da Vinci Code.

The fact that these ideas were initially explored and explained within The Holy Blood and the Holy Grail was not something that Dan Brown regarded as an issue. Dan Brown even went so far as to name one of the major characters in The Da Vinci Code after the authors of The Holy Blood and the Holy Grail. Leigh Teabing takes his first name from Richard Leigh, while his surname is an agrammatical form of Baigent. It's a salute to any person who has read about The Priory of Sion before. In a novel with an underlying plot that relies on clues hidden in many works that Brown created, his puzzle is relatively straightforward to understand. The idea was never intended to be kept secret.

However, during the trial, Dan Brown and his publishers' legal team argued that the author actually had no knowledge of the subject apart from the information his wife gave him. The judge noted that it was not of any interest to Brown what the process of research for the book was dealt with. However, Peter Smith seemed content to accept to the fact that Dan Brown had taken his wife's work and incorporated it into his novel, content to have his wife's research expertise.

Although this could indicate an insufficient amount of thoroughness regarding the accuracy of historical facts in The Da Vinci Code, this did seem to be somewhat in conflict with the statements that were made by Dan Brown following the trial. After the judge handed down the verdict and handed over his case Brown and his publisher, Brown came out to state that he felt the outcome was a victory on behalf of "artistic expressiveness." It was crucial that he informed the media that the novelist was at ease drawing on any aspect of history they wanted to without fear of being sued by any other person.

This leaves us with a variety of concerns. Apart from the questionable value given to The Da Vinci Code as an exceptional piece of art and a masterpiece, we have to consider the question of just what extent we should consider the theories of The Holy Blood and the Holy Grail to be considered as historical? The answer will become apparent over the length of this book The very concept behind being the Priory of Sion is up to discussion. It is believed that the priory's history can be traced back for thousands of years, however there are some who suggest that its fame ended the day it was founded in the London courtroom. If we ask the question: what specifically are Sion's Priory of Sion, we have to ask ourselves: what exactly is the best way for us to accurately describe something as a verifiable piece of the past?

In the present today, The Priory of Sion is big business. When we look back to The Da Vinci Code, we will see a novel which was subsequently optioned to be made into a movie. The film was directed by Ron Howard and with Tom Hanks as the main character the film was a success enough to earn its sequels. Angels and Demons was released following the film, and Inferno is scheduled to release in the year 2016. In addition to the money at the box office that the film earned it was able to stir into the debate over the subject matter of the book over again. The topic, it appears to be extremely turbulent. When we look at the development of the concept to The three writers of The Holy Blood and the Holy Grail This is the reason for the media hype that has been steadily increasing throughout the years.

What is the reason that it would cause nations to prohibit the film? In India For instance the film was condemned and banned for casting doubt on the divine nature and divinity of Jesus Christ. Christianity is the biggest religion around the globe and Catholicism the most popular religious denomination. What idea could be that is presented in a few films and books, have the same impact?

It could be that the answer lies in one of the authors in The Holy Blood and the Holy Grail. Three authors wrote the book, and it is the author has been barely mentioned who could provide an opening point to the story of the Priory of Sion, the lens through which the majority of the story that follows will be understood. The name is Henry Lincoln. In all the characters of the story, he's possibly the only reason people from the English spoken world have heard about the Priory. Perhaps he is the reason you read this book in the first place. The difference isthat his name isn't well-known to the general population. However, that's not to suggest that he's not well-known or recognized.

We'll take a minute to examine the opening for The Da Vinci Code. Before we get into the story of Henry Lincoln, we should be aware that anyone who started the most popular novel received a message by the author. Before the novel had even began, and before the reader begins to get involved in the story the author had included an introduction to read. The book is placed in an overall context. It begins with one important word: facts. Through the entire book there will be plot holes as well as unexpected shocks. Albino monks will whip themselves , and characters will cross-check each other. All of this takes place in the popular world of fiction. When you read a novel, you're well aware that what you're reading may not be true. It is that, unless of course the author is willing to claim contrary. In the instance of Dan Brown, there is an assertion of "fact" in the first chapter of the book that provides readers with information about the world they are about to enter.

"Fact," Dan Brown writes, "The Priory of Sion [...] is a genuine institution." Brown continues to refer to a variety of sources from the past (which we'll discuss in the future) to support making his point however, he leaves readers with no doubt that the Priory is in fact a real place. In addition to the art works that are featured throughout the novel, as well as other evidence of historical fact, as well as the more zany elements of the story, Brown makes it clear to audience on the fact that his Priory of Sion is a genuine organization, one that will prove to be extremely significant in the next novel. It's this type of assessment and assurance that is required to understand prior to meeting Henry Lincoln. Without Lincoln there would be no one who could be as certain about anything. The authors Baigent and Leigh will be adamant about the manner that Brown provides the preface to his novel. While they might not agree on the subject in court, the information in that sentence is very much similar to the information they provided in their book The Holy Blood and the Holy Grail. The third writer in this book, who was not in the courtroom is Henry Lincoln. In the sequel to their best-selling work that was non-fiction The Messianic

Legacy, three authors wrote that the details about The Priory of Sion that they exposed was enough to shake the "very foundations of Christianity." Similar to like Dan Brown, Lincoln and his co-authors were more than content to defend the validity that was the Priory. If all this was a measurable facts, If Lincoln and his co-authors put so much work into their book If the information contained included in The Da Vinci Code was only a few accepted facts Then what was it that made the Catholic Church so enraged by the book of Dan Brown? Why did the world not be aware of Sion Priory? Priory of Sion? And how did the three authors find the secret information?

While he wasn't at the time of his trial of London, Henry Lincoln was the source for the understanding of the Priory of Sion that we are able to access to this day. Being an author on The Holy Blood and the Holy Grail You might be expecting to see him along with Baigent or Leigh. However, Henry Lincoln was never exactly what he appeared to be. For some -- especially in the 1980s, Henry Lincoln was more well-known as a TV personality. He would appear on the odd show, covering the history of the time and hosting informative shows. At times, the writer would come up with something that was close to serious content. Affectionate, relaxed and friendly He stood out from the pompous television historians who were before his. In a turtleneck sweatshirt and sporting a loose beard around his head, he dealt with numerous questions or discoveries wearing a laid-back but plausible demeanor. For a specific generation of TV viewers the man was a major departure from the past and was a fascinating character on the scene of television history.

It's not the complete reality regarding Henry Lincoln, however. If we look deeper into his life, we discover numerous things that aren't so simple as they appear. First it is true that his real name is Henry Soskin. There are many people working in the entertainment business change their names after they are famous. However, what's interesting to note is Henry Lincoln (or Soskin) wasn't actually historian. He was a actor as well as a writer and had been working in the world of television for quite a while. As as a writer, he been involved in numerous science fiction series which included the well-known BBC show Doctor Who. If you search at his name can come across that it appears in the film credits for a film from 1968 featuring Boris Karloff called The Curse of the Crimson Altar. Henry Lincoln was a co-writer of the film. As an actor as well as a writer one could take it as an established fact that he knew how to create a narrative.

Henry Lincoln's most memorable story was repeated over and over and to ever more influential people. It started with a celebration. He was in 1969 and, as he recalled in the preface of The Holy Blood and the Holy Grail the time the journey he took towards the southern part of France. On the route, he decided the book he wanted to purchase. He started looking for an e-book -- something lighter to read during a holidayand he bought a novel named The Accursed Treasure. The novel is written in French and was written by a man whose name was Gerard de Sede. According to Lincoln who read it, it is "lightweight" in its simplicity and "entertaining." This book was able to mix elements of factual history along with "genuine mysterious" with a hint of speculation. The story revolved around a priest from an isolated town in the 19th century France. The priest resided in Rennes-le-Chateau in a very poor area of Languedoc and also had a poor church. However, one day, as according to the book to have revealed an astonishing secret in the church. The revelation was enough to make the priest an extremely wealthy person and his church was greatly benefited.

The Accursed Treasure stayed for Henry Lincoln. While most people have read it once, and then forget about it but something about the tale that of the poor man who struck it lucky stuck with the man. However, there was one issue. The book stated that the discovery that the priest made was based on "cryptic document," the book didn't provide the specifics of what the documents were. They were also included in the book however the author did not give any explanation. Two documents that were said to be found in the church that were included in the book, but it was difficult to determine the exact meaning of these documents. They had to be decoded and a fact that clung on the inside of Lincoln's skull as an ostrich.

Armed with the two unsettling documents he discovered in the book Henry Lincoln set about trying to figure out their significance. After a few minutes the man even succeeded. But it wasn't enough. If it was that simple to Lincoln and he had just two pages of notes from the elusive discovery, then why had Gerard de Sede not deciphered the notes by himself? For Lincoln it was just adding an element of mystery. After he had solved the mystery of the two first sheets, Henry was becoming more obsessed by the tale. Not only was he required to unravel the other papers and documents, but he also needed to inform more people about the mysterious documents and the meaning they carried. As he dug into the deeper levels to uncover the secrets, new "layers of significance" started to be revealed to the writer.

Armed with these glimpses into the occult universe, Henry Lincoln set about disseminating his message. He was a TV industry which made it natural to go directly to the most powerful authority within his own business - the BBC. BBC was the British Broadcasting Corporation produced a vast array of documentary and historical programs. They even had a regularly-scheduled program that was devoted to such problems. The show was titled Chronicle. In spite of the fact Henry Lincoln was neither an academic historian nor an experienced Anthropologist however, the BBC believed it was a good story to tell. They asked Henry to write an article that would be aired in the show Chronicle which when you think about his lack of qualifications is quite impressive. Perhaps even more impressive that Lincoln was able to convince television executives even though he was armed with just two copies of pages from a flimsy French paperback.

It is as amazing as it could appear, Henry Lincoln received his funds and packed his things and headed off to France. A meeting in Paris with Gerard de Sede was arranged. He was the writer of The Accursed Treasure was set to meet with Lincoln in Paris during the last month of 1970. While the meeting appeared to be an informal affair, Lincoln could not help from asking de Sede as to why it was not his intention to give full explanations of the whole text. After being forced into submission and apprehensively, the Frenchman responded in a manner that Lincoln kept throughout the rest of his life. The decryptions weren't provided, de Sede exclaimed, just because "we thought it might be of interest to anyone like you to learn the answers for themselves."

The French writer could not be more wrong. Lincoln was, as he could see was already hooked. The chance of discovering more information was similar to an addiction that the British man had already been offered an experience. De Sede began to supply tiny bits of information, drip-feeding the truth about the tiny church in the tiny town. This was not just the one code that required to be broken, it appeared. Lincoln was able to plunge further and further down the rabbit hole. The first mystery that were revealed to him was one of the most famous artists in the world, the French artist Poussin. According to the writer in The Accursed Treasure, there was a tomb hidden inside the French countryside, which bore striking resemblances to one in the Poussin painting The Shepherds of Arcadia. It was found close to the Church in Rennes-le-Chateau located in a location known as Pontils. De Sede even had photographs. When he presented them to Lincoln his photos, the resemblance was evident and stunning. Lincoln started to think there was something more than an urban legend. What he called an "small small local mystery" began to take shape into "unexpected size."

The unexpected dimension resulted in the fact that there would eventually be three installments of the Chronicle series. Unsatisfied with only one piece of content, Lincoln helped to produce two more about the church in Rennes-le-Chateau. The first was titled The Lost Treasure of Jerusalem and was broadcast in 1972. Following a favorable reception the show was followed by 1974's The Priest, the Painter and the Devil. The first two episodes were a hit with the British public of television. Like de Sede's novel the series featured a delightful mixture of code to decode the mysteries of the past and hidden histories, buried treasures, and an intriguing idea. According to the film the secrets to unravelling the mystery lay in artwork. Find the solution in artwork, and you'll assist in unravelling the mystery. Similar to the tomb of the Poussin painting the secrets of the church were apparently known to artists.

The most notable thing missing on this show is any kind of criticism, particularly at the serious end of the spectrum of historians. The show is telecast on the BBC it is reasonable to think that the show would be a strict adherent to a certain set of guidelines. There was no one with a complaint about the lack of in the historical significance of the shows by Lincoln. Because they were short and were well-liked by the majority of the population, maybe nobody thought they were too significant. It's not worth getting riled up about. In the days of clumsy video recorders, and no internet meant that once a program was broadcast, repeated viewings were not easy to do. There was no sense to be agitated over an event that was broadcast on Chronicle. There was no need for historians or any members of the Catholic Church felt it necessary to react to Lincoln's findings.

Following the airing of the first episode of the Chronicle series, Henry Lincoln found his team was growing. The first time, Lincoln had to work with Michael Baigent and Richard Leigh. Richard Leigh had been the first to join Lincoln's world. They had both been lecturing at an academic summer camp for writers in the year 1975. In a down time, they were discussing The Knights Templar along with other mysteries. The conversation turned to films Lincoln was shooting, and Leigh provided his assistance to Lincoln should he require any clarification regarding the issue concerning the Templars. Furthermore, Leigh provided the introduction to Baigent who was a graduate of psychology who had renounced an extremely lucrative career as photographer for an agency for news in order to pursue his passion for everything related to his love for the Knights Templar.

The trio collaborated for first time in what would ultimately be the third installment into Lincoln's Lincoln's film series for

Chronicle. The film was called The Shadow of the Templars and was released in 1979. In the words of Leigh the short films were seen as by BBC as the "most successful documentaries that the BBChas ever produced." Additionally was the work that the three did on the final installment of the series gave them details that could help to unravel the mystery surrounding that church located in Rennes-le-Chateau. The collaboration they put into in the making of the documentary Chronicle was to form the basis for The Holy Blood and the Holy Grail.

Anyone who managed to watch the very first episode in the Lincoln series produced by the BBC may remember the last lines of the show. In the introduction of The Holy Blood and the Holy Grail, Lincoln was sure that "something special is waiting to be discovered" within the church. The book that three men wrote was a way to find out what that extraordinary thing was. When the book went out on sale the public was equally fascinated. This was so much, in fact that on the very initial day of publication, the book was sold out in 43,000 copies.

In spite of having no background in the subject, and using an obscure part of French fiction, Henry Lincoln had put in place the elements which would later become our understanding of the Priory of Sion. It's certain that if Lincoln chosen not to go on vacation in southern France and instead stayed in France, the Priory could not have been well-known. With so many assertions being made about the shocking secrets that were revealed in the Church of Rennes-le-Chateau It could be the right time to look into the reason The Holy Blood and the Holy Grail was such bestseller.

Chapter 2: The Secrets Of The Holy Blood And The Holy Grail

In the book, we've repeatedly referred in the past to The Holy Blood and the Holy Grail without spending much time looking at what these books are trying to achieve. It is true that the Priory of Sion remains tied to this book and no discussion of the Priory and their purpose could be complete without having a look at some of the concepts that are presented through Henry Lincoln, Michael Baigent along with Richard Leigh.

There is a major thesis of the book that can be understood by anyone that has ever read The Da Vinci Code. The theory has been discussed numerous times in the book, but let's have a moment to explore the concept in detail.

Simply put, The Holy Blood and the Holy Grail implies that there exists a secret society dubbed The Priory of Sion. The Priory's origins back to 1099 and was governed at different times by a group of famous and well-known individuals who all have the title of Grand Master. The prior Grand Masters have included Leonardo Da

Vinci and Isaac Newton, and that the goal the secret society has is return the Merovingian family into the French throne as well in spreading the influence that is the Merovingian family throughout Europe. It is believed that the Priory is of the belief that the Merovingian lineage is sacred and holds secrets that can change the world.

The book also suggests the book that different societies and, in particular, those of the Knights Templar -- owe their existence to the work of the Priory. The book claims the Templars were created in the Crusades as a type of financial and military department within the Priory of Sion. Through the Templars they were able to ensure that the Priory could display a kind of power without having to disclose themselves or put their secrets in danger. This is also the basis of The Holy Blood and the Holy Grail.

It is said it is believed that Jesus Christ, the founder of Christianity (and an important figure in many various other religions) was married by Mary Magdalene. This is not all, the union produced a lot of children. From the children, it is easy to determine the lineage of Jesus Christ from his death to the present day. Following the execution and arrest by Jesus Christ, the authors believe that Mary Magdalene and her children left across the Near East and settled in southern France. They were married there with a variety of significant noble families. This resulted in the rise of Merovingian King of the Merovingian. This led to the rise of Merovingian kings. Priory of Sion believes that this bloodline needs to be safeguarded at all costs.

This is connected to the concept that there is a Holy Grail. An item that has been around for a long time and is that is of great importance to Western Christendom The Holy Grail has been described in various ways as a cup or chalice, which when drunk from -- will give you eternal life. It has been featured in films and literature from the era of the medieval French poems to the Indiana Jones film franchise. The writers in The Holy Blood and the Holy Grail assert they believe that The Holy Grail is not a physical cup. It is instead an ode in two ways. The first is Mary Magdalene's womb who gave birth to those children born to Jesus. The second is in the lineage of Jesus's descendents. We will discover this in a moment the belief is that an error was made in telling the story changed the character of the grail, changing it from a symbolic reference to a metaphysical object into a physical object. The search for this Holy Grail is actually a search for the truth regarding Jesus Christ's lineage. Jesus Christ. According to the Bible that he wrote, his descendants are still walking through the earth to this day.

These theories weren't taken out of thin air. In the course of their investigation, Lincoln and his fellow writers came upon documents known as the Dossiers Secrets, a collection of documents believed to be ancient which were hidden within the National Library of France. The documents were believed to provide authors with an extensive background of the Merovingian lineage. They incorporated this information with their understanding about and understanding of Roman Catholic Church, as along with their knowledge of the past and their previous work accomplished in Rennes-le-Chateau. They believed that the dynasties described by Dossiers Secrets Dossiers Secrets demonstrated how the bloodline of the lineage went through towards Mary Magdalene, but they believed they could use this information to prove it was possible to trace the bloodline back to David, the King. David.

According to The Holy Blood and the Holy Grail The Priory of Sion exists in conjunction with this knowledge regarding those who are children of Jesus Christ. It is the duty to the Priory to safeguard and assist the lineage. But who exactly do they need to defend themselves against? In the text, it's it is the Catholic Church that assumes the character of the villain. In the book, the authors explain how they feel that the Catholic Church is threatening people who descend from Christ. They have not only destroyed organizations like that of Knights Templar (and the Cathars) which were established to protect descendants as well, but they've attempted to murder several bloodline members. The reason? Power.

The Catholic Church, as per The Holy Blood and the Holy Grail hopes to keep the authority of the throne of the episcopal throne. In other words, the Pope serves as the spokesperson of God in the world of Earth. If a descendant from Jesus Christ himself remain alive this would put the power of God in grave danger.

The Priory of Sion with a list of objectives. The authors can draw the conclusion (after studying the evidence they have) that this Priory should be devoted to various causes and all with the aim to protect the child who are the children of Jesus Christ and Mary Magdalene.

The first goal is to expose to everyone the tomb of Sigebert IV as well as the elusive precious treasures from the Jerusalem Temple. These are believed to be the true physical records that trace the lineage that belong to Jesus Christ. They offer a convincing evidence that Jesus had children and that the children are still alive to the present times. The history of these things is tied with the rise of Charlemagne the French King who overthrew Merovingian Dynasty.

The other is to encourage the development of a type of pan-European pride. It is connected to the revival of chivalry, a moral code that was popularized for its use by the medieval French knights. The Priory believe that the increase in knightly chivalry will result in an improved Europe in the near future however this is one of the assertions that is usually dismissed when talking about The Holy Blood and the Holy Grail.

The third goal is linked with the rise of the an ecclesiastical order and the pan-European feeling of nationalists. The Priory wants to create the concept of a United States of Europe, with all of it under the banner of one religion. The Holy European Empire will be established and governed with the Merovingian (and therefore holy) bloodline. It will also involve the union of places of religious and political power. In the end, the Holy See is set to be removed and at his place the descendant of Jesus will take over the political and spiritual leadership.

In the end, the people who wrote the text believedafter these goals had been achieved, The Priory of Sion would be capable of taking on the role of a central government that extends across Europe. This would mean the creation of a one-party state government, which will give to the Priory with the sole source of actual power.

The further one deviates from the underlying premise of the text and the further it falls to the world of conventional conspiracy theories. There had been earlier theories about the existence of Christ's children (and the fact that they were born of Mary Magdalene), The Holy Blood and the Holy Grail was believed to have been the first book that combined these ideas with equally broad ideas about European power struggle.

This could be due to the fact that the authors included a widely documented document on conspiracies in their investigation. It is known by the name The Protocols of the Elders of Zion The document is suspicious of both Masons and Jews. It has been described as anti-Semitic as well as anti-Masonic. For Lincoln and the other writers the concepts outlined in the document appeared to be in line with what they discovered in their studies into the background of the Priory of Sion. They even went further. The text says that The Protocols of the Elders of Zion was the most revealing source of evidence regarding the activities of the Priory. The Priory believed the initial document (the one that had served as the basis for The Protocols of the Elders of Zion) was no connection with or had anything to do with relate to Judaism and had been issued by Masons (specifically those who were practicing their Scottish Rite) and the use of the word "Zion' was not really an indication of Judaism (as the text was perceived) however it was an allusion towards The Priory of Sion. The Priory of Sion was actually the Priory that was the Masons believed were responsible for a worldwide conspiracy but rather than their fellow Jewish people.

Baigent, Lincoln, and Leigh were believed they were right. The Protocols of the Elders of Zion was not meant to be available to the general public. Instead, it simply outlined the ways in which writers and the readers could wrest over the control of the Freemasons in order to destabilize and reform the church and the state. The alteration towards the direction that The Protocols was made following the failure of a mission to gain influence at the Russian court. Serge Nilus altered the text and published the text in 1903 with the intention to denigrate and discredit the Catholic Church. The men who were surrounded by the Pope were, as it was believed to suggest, were in fact Jewish or Masonic conspirators, who were put in the positions of authority. By ignoring the obscure Christian values so closely to that of the Priory of Sion, Nilus was able to dissociate the text from its initial purpose, leaving people throughout the centuries with a distorted understanding of its original meaning. The writers suggest that it was the Priory of Sion faded purposefully in the background.

The entire book is presented in almost 500 text pages. It is supported by 37 pages of footnotes, comments as well as 24 pages of illustrations and photos, as well an extensive bibliography that includes the texts that are available in English, German, and French. Although the cover could make it appear like an action novel, the inside is clearly focused on academic credibility, and will go to great lengths to provide the reality of the assertions. However, there's a plethora of populism in the story that's not typically found in academic work. Consider, for instance, the manner in which the story is presented.

Jesus Mary Magdalene and Jesus have been described as being lovers. According to some, this is supported by the ancient scrolls (though they are in reality they're books) that were found at the time of their discovery in Egypt in 1945. They've been called The Gnostic Gospels. However, they claim that they believe that the relation between Jesus and Mary did not come without issues. According to the authors, Peter was a disciple of Jesus and the one who would later found the Catholic Church and eventually become the first Pope was insecure. He was not a fan of the closeness by the pair. After Jesus was executed, Mary fled across the water and hid along with her family. They are being protected in the community of the Jewish community in southern part of France. Already the story is beginning to look like a play rather than an academic paper.

The story continues four hundred years later when the Merovingian line starts to ascend to prominence. The French monarchs eventually are overthrown to the side of Carolingians as well as Charlemagne as well as the bloodline that carries Jesus the Messiah is again and forced to hide. The descendants of Jesus change into French aristocratsknown as known as the House of Lorraine. If they have a member of the house, Godfrey de Bouillon, participates in the first Crusade and is given with the crown that was taken from the Holy Lands. He is one of the first Christian to be crowned King of Jerusalem for a long time (if the day ever comes). However, the unnoticed hand that has guided his climb to the highest point is his own Priory of Sion. The secret society has yet to name after the coronation, however, shortly after their coronation they began to establish a small monastery at

Mount Zion in the captured city. The name they choose is that is the Priory of Sion. When they begin to build the Knights Templar They begin excavating Solomon's Temple. They discover an undiscovered treasure hidden beneath the floor. It could represent the remains Jesus Christ or the Ark of the Covenant. It could be even the documents that prove Christ's descendants exist.

The Priory remain a formidable (though obscure) power to reckon with for centuries. It was not until the year 1307, that they Catholic Church finally takes an attempt to eradicate them. In 1307, when they watch the French monarchy (worried about the existence of the existence of a Merovingian bloodline) and the Catholic Church (worried about threats to their authority over religious law) collaborate against the Priory in an attempt to take on the public authorities. In the end, Knights Templar is disbanded, its members are rounded up and are beaten. The Templars according to the Church to be devil-loving usurpers. With their great military and banking institutions The Priory of Sion flees from the public eye. They possess their most crucial secret - that of Jesus Christ -- and they are determined to protect the truth at all costs.

A most intriguing aspects of the book but it's the way it asserts the existence of clues, hints and clues to the truth behind the Priory were left in numerous pieces of art scattered throughout Europe. For the hundreds of years after the Knights Templar were first prosecuted in the year 1215, the Priory has made a point of leaving clues regarding the truth behind medieval and Renaissance artworks, sculptures and tapestries. Perhaps the most well-known of these is the tale of the Grail the Grail itself. According to the text (and in a myth which gives the book its name) the expression that is now known as Holy Grail (San Graal) is in fact a reference to the traditional cup. It is from this that the symbol of the cup which confers immortality originated. It was also believed to be the cup Jesus took a drink from during the table at the end of the meal. The authors argue that this is an incorrect interpretation of the facts. In reality, San Graal is Sang Real. A letter moves from the beginning of a word to the next. There is a slight distinction in spelling. Simple mistakes prior to the invention to the printing press. Also, and most importantly, even though San Graal may have been the cup of the past, Sang Real means holy blood. The divine lineage. Children of Jesus Christ. The answer, Priory historians say, is in a well-known painting. Leonardo da Vinci knew the truth about the Holy Grail, which is why his representation of the Last Supper is not depicted with an empty cup on the table right in front of Jesus Christ. Such clues are designed to let the world know the truth, but without being explicit.

The book suggests that this fascinating story and astonishing secrets are passed on over generations. In the following 700 years the Priory of Sion recruited the most brilliant and intelligent minds of their generation with the help by a number of Masters. They shared the secrets of Jesus Mary Magdalene and Jesus as well as guarding the descendants of the couple. This is the list of the Grand Masters that the team of Henry Lincoln, Michael Baigent as well as Richard

Leigh discovered in the National Library of France, in Dossiers Secrets. Dossiers Secrets. The list is a list of the top names in European science and art. Victor Hugo. Isaac Newton. Claude Debussy. Jean Cocteau. Robert Boyle. Leonardo da Vinci.

The way in which these ideas are presented in a non-academic and exciting way makes it simple to understand the reason The Holy Blood and the Holy Grail was a huge success. The information that it appears to impart to its readers hints at an ancient conspiracy that completely redefines the way we think about European history as well as about the most popular religion on earth and the present situation of geopolitics. It's an amazing story that is written almost like an action movie. The reader is even involved.

We've already mentioned that the investigations of Henry Lincoln involved the creation of a painting of Nicolas Poussin. In the painting, The Shepherds of Arcadia, it is stated, contains the remains of a tomb. The side of the grave, the artist spent the time to write the words "Et in the Arcadia Ego which is a clue that Poussin knew well.

This practice of sprinkling clues on artworks is catching on with Priory however. We know that the year 1885 was when a clergyman from the tiny south-western French town Rennes-le-Chateau suddenly accumulated an enormous amount of money. The priest, who was named Berenger Sauniere, is said to have found out an pillar that he had in his church was actually hollow. When he opened it to look inside, he saw a host of documents encrypted inside. With the help of the local bishop and a local bishop, he attempted to break the codes and found the secret message:

"To Dagobert II [the last of the Merovingian Kings] as king, and to Sion is this treasure, and the treasure is in Sion, where he died."
The message was insignificant to anything, however Sauniere realized it was a reference to Jesus Christ's lineage. Jesus Christ. With this information (and another proof was discovered inside the column) and he was in a position to blackmail his way into the Catholic Church. The priest was

rewarded with some money that he used to renovate the once poor and deplorable church and decorating the interior with clearly un-Christian symbols.

To summarize it, it was on the discovery of Gerard de Sede began to write his novel. After that, the book was was read by Henry Lincoln. Then the BBC requested the creation of the stories for Chronicle. This brought Lincoln into contact to Baigent as well as Leigh. The result was the discovery of documents found in the National Library of France. This resulted in the creation of The Holy Blood and the Holy Grail.

The last stage of the depiction by the authors of Priory of Sion was perhaps the most outrageous. After years of doing studies and finding the entirety of the parts that were put together to form The Holy Blood and the Holy Grail, they hinted about the name of the current Grand Master. The person who is currently in charge of Sion's Priory of Sion, they believed, was Pierre Plantard de St Clair. Pierre it was believed that he was a direct descendent from the Merovingian lineage and was a heir of the French throne. Also, he was the personification of the bloodline of Jesus Christ. The reason the information began to be revealed as the book stated was due to the fact that Plantard was in the process of starting his political career, leading a group that could change the course of world politics forever. What was the future for Plantard however, the authors were unable to declare.

The centuries-old mystery outlined in the text by its authors guides the reader to the point where they're flipping through the pages and with the book in their hands. The book involves the reader and in the midst of a long-running conspiracy.

The Holy Blood and the Holy Grail not only provides an exciting plot on the past of the Catholic Church, but it effortlessly draws the reader into the family. With a clever approach, Baigent, Leigh, and Lincoln succeed in making their own search for truth more interesting readers. By the fact of being aware of their involvement in the Priory of Sion, the authors make the reader a part of the plot. This book is intriguing on a variety of levels, and explains the reason why this book will become so popular, particularly considering that other historical non-fiction books do not sell as well. It could be the result of Blythe Brown grabbing one of the books and passing the details her husband. This would lead to two authors appearing in an London courtroom and accusing a fictional writer of plagiarism. This is, without doubt the primary reason for the interest you have in Sion's Priory today. Priory of Sion today. However, that's not to say that the work had no critics. The next section we'll begin to delve deeper into the intricacies within the text and the way it connects the pieces. As we do we'll be able to see the truth behind Sion's Priory. Priory of Sion.

Chapter 3: The Royal Bloodline

It could be a surprise to readers of today to find out the fact that The Holy Blood and the Holy Grail was not immediately attacked by reviewers. In the modern age of instant communications and a world-wide internet, a book of this kind could be expected to provoke anger across the globe The fires are fueled due to the accessibility of information. In the 1980s, however there was a lively but largely uninterested response to the theories proposed in the book by its authors.

There were some who were not enthused by the ideas. Hugh Montefiore, for example served as the Anglican Bishop in Birmingham at the moment of the publication and appeared on television to talk about the book. On the program were the writers themselves. Both parties were involved in a sort of a debate about the real story of the book. However, since it was the show was telecast on late-night television, and featuring the participation of a British priest as well as writers and authors, the debate did not get too heated.

In other places, there were positive responses. In the papers of the time the literary critics seemed to take pleasure in the unique glimpse into a previously unexplored world. The Times Educational Supplement, for instance, described the book as "compulsive reading" and The Oxford Times described the book as being packed with "well documented and often shady information." However, there were discordant opinions from the media. The Times Literary Supplement (in an independent review addressed to their Educational group) declared the book "rather ridiculous" and deemed it to constitute "worthless." The book seemed to be some recognition of how difficult the concepts could be and being the Sunday Telegraph concluding that the book will surely "infuriate several ecclesiastical leaders," even if it did acknowledge that the authors could be proved right.

Even in America which was located on the other part of the Atlantic the public was paying attention to the book. Even though the Chronicle series was not airing within the United States at the time some newspapers like that of the Los Angeles Times reviewed the book and said that the book had more than enough in the book to "challenge the conventional Christian convictions."

Reviews like these made huge differences in the way the work was perceived. In book stores, there is an enormous difference between books that are inside the New Age or Spiritual section or Spiritual section, and those that are placed in the category of the past. Although The Holy Blood and the Holy Grail could be assumed to be in the first, because of the unqualified history credibility of the authors, the publicity regarding the book resulted in it was moved to the second section of the bookshop. Being in the historical section gave it the possibility of a certain cache as well as an expectation of a thorough investigation and truthfulness by those who were perusing the shelves. The book appeared to be so enthralled with ancient mysteries and conspiracy theories, The Holy Blood and the Holy Grail didn't get the same skepticism that is usually applied to novels about alien abductions or the disappearing cities of Atlantis. It was regarded as to be a serious investigation into the history of the world and that the presence of the Priory of Sion was taken to be grounded in clear, well-studied historical facts. In the end, it sold hundreds of thousand copies.

In the wake of the huge success that was The Holy Blood and the Holy Grail The authors decided to write not only an individual, but rather a large variety of sequels in different media. We've already talked about The Messianic Legacy (the book's sequel) that came out within three years however there were several others, all written by the three authors, or by them individually. They were titled The Dead Sea Scrolls Deception and The Elixir and the Stone. Henry Lincoln took a special interest in the church of Rennes-le-Chateau and began to create guides including videos, maps as well as lectures and various other resources specifically focusing on the church.

Following the cult success in The Holy Blood and the Holy Grail The Holy Blood and the Holy Grail, there was a tsunami of media and merchandise on the same themes as the book's original. This isn't just exclusive to the three original authors. Just typing in Mary Magdalene on Google will provide you with a multitude of sources that claim to have all the facts about the Biblical character. This is the case for those who believe in the Holy Grail, the Knights Templar and a myriad of other figures connected to Sion's Priory of Sion. In the end, it is now a huge business.

Additionally people who have had an enduring success publishing books about these topics have realized the potential for riches and sales that are far above what historians of the average think of. This isn't just about books as well as CD-ROMs, DVDs and, more recently, YouTube videos, which all make up an entire new set of priory-related media that could nearly guarantee a return from your investments. It can be traced back to the original popularity in The Holy Blood and the Holy Grail. In a way, a work that is focused on trace the history of a notable historical figure could be traced back through the span of nearly forty years. The book you're reading now has a connection to the achievements of Baigent, Leigh, and Lincoln. And that's not forgetting the phenomenal popularity in The Da Vinci Code.

However, all this success was accompanied by the added benefit of judging. Richard Leigh and Michael Baigent weren't historians, nor were Henry Lincoln (though he did portray one on TV). In the wake from the impressive sales figures and the increasing curiosity about The Holy Grail, the Priory of Sion and the theories outlined within The Holy Blood and the Holy Grail, it should be expected to expect that academic credibility of these authors would soon be scrutinized. As a result the possibility of criticism could be opened. When people began to consider seriously the ideas that shaped the book, was it capable of standing up? Did the research conducted into the book sufficient to ensure that the Priory precisely as they written about it?

For those who watched the Chronicle series on television , or those who bought The

Holy Blood and the Holy Grail from the history section of the bookshop There was a belief in the level of rigor used in the research of Henry Lincoln and his cohorts. It is a fundamental social contract that assumes that whenever a piece of information appears in this way that it is in line with the academic principles of history. The other items the Chronicle Chronicle have been written, edited and edited by highly qualified historians. Other books in the store could also have been written by skilled individuals. To the extent that they were the new wave of media included an account of the Priory of Sion as part of the same archive of historical research one would think of. It was just more engaging than typical kind of film, and presented as the kind of fictitious thriller.

It could be assumed it was the case that the author of this work had stumbled upon interesting stories within their usual course of research, it soon was evident that they were attracted by, let's say, non-orthodox ideas of Christianity. The areas they were interested in such as the beginnings of the Church as well as research into the Bible,

Freemasonry, alchemy, Renaissance art, myths stories, legends, and secrecy societies were definitely outside the norm of investigation into the past. However, if it was to be believed that the authors adhered to the established research practices and methods, there is no problem with this. In fact the writers should be praised for making history fascinating and relevant to our current society.

Therein lies the issue. Three authors who wrote The Holy Blood and the Holy Grail didn't hold their work to the standards that were accepted. They were aware of what is expected by researchers within the realm of the study of history and they did not adhere to those rules. The book lays out this within their work. Instead of defending themselves from these claims, the trio decided to embrace their denial of historical accuracy. Alongside discovering what was true regarding The Priory of Sion and the truth about the Holy Grail, it seemed that the trio believed that they had discovered a completely new method to view the past.

It is enough to look over some of the more boring sections of The Holy Blood and the

Holy Grail. Although there are portions of the text that deal with hidden societies and plots inside the Catholic Church However, there are sections that aren't as captivating. One could be forgiven to glance over the sections of the text that the authors examine the "sorely insufficient" methods they believe constitute "academic study." In the next paragraph they explain their conviction that they were required to drop "conventional analysis" when they tried to establish any "requisite connections" that connect the "radically various sources of subject matter" they decided to study. This means that they did not think they had to verify their work against the academic standards, just because of the subject matter they were examining.

As we'll see in the following paragraphs it is a important and significant admission that will determine the manner we see Sion as a Priory of Sion, and the way in which it is perceived by the outside world. It could also provide a clue about how a book was able to be so popular in comparison to other works in the field. In fact, a quick glance of the text where the quotes above were derived would only serve to provide the reader with several important phrases. These could include "academic," "conventional," or "scholarship," all of that would suggest an even higher academic credentials than the ones actually utilized. Once the true significance of the sentence is understood the uninitiated reader is already absorbed in fascinating stories of Catholic conspiracy theories.

The argument for the absence of scholarly theories in the research is claimed to be due to the topic itself. Because that the Priory of Sion was counter to the traditional narrative of history The writers suggest that their study should not be required to be based on the standard criteria that historical narratives are evaluated. There was hardly any previously published material that they could investigate, as they were innovating. The authors paint an image that encapsulates for people who read their book that their interpretation of events is a risky radical. Any criticism of the theories that came from the old guard, or from the traditional academic would be obvious. It's like a conspiracy. By making a point about the lack of standards in the study, critics are put in the camp of evil. This made any critique of the book extremely difficult. For the writers in The Holy Blood and the Holy Grail novelists, the novelist has more freedom than historians. Whereas the historian is constrained and confined by academic discipline but the novelist is free to dream, speculate and chase even the most insignificant of leads. This made Baigent, Leigh, and Lincoln into detectives, affluent men who navigate through dangerous waters to find the truth. This made the subsequent accusations leveled towards Dan Brown all the stranger. It was precisely this kind of atmosphere and the way in which they approached their work that enabled the writers to express their ideas and remain largely free of criticism.

What do these mean to the author? What, more importantly, is it implying for the theories that the book proposes? A thorough study of The Holy Blood and the Holy Grail will result in you are often confronted with phrases like "if" or "probable." You can look at any section in The Holy Blood and the Holy Grail, the style of prose will keep on this manner. Once you have pointed it out, it's impossible to remove this thought from the brain. It is important to keep in mind this fact: Lincoln and Leigh each had a long background in writing fiction. Their writing styles were not academic. Highly skilled writers, they be able to convey an idea in a proper manner. With their careful use of the language of writing, as writers they are able to write in what could be described as a pretentious style. The author makes leaps of faith and assumptions are made. However, the clever writing conceals the issue at the first sight.

These beliefs appear at first glance to be completely sensible. For instance, Henry Lincoln asks the reader to think about two ideas. The first is that a man was born to an unmarried woman and was capable of walking on the water's surface and, following his execution -was raised to life. Second, the person was born and was married, and then raised the family of his wife. Which is the more plausible scenario, Lincoln asks the reader to decide which is more likely to be the case? If the reader appears to assume that the second is more likely to be true as it's most likely scenario to be the case, Lincoln then uses this to back the argument.

This is an ineffective method. For instance, take the gospels. In these chapters of the Bible the reader is told the account of a man that was born to an unmarried woman, who did walk on water, and returned to the world. While it is a questionable assumption they may seem but they are found in the primary scriptures in the Christian faith. The notions formulated by Lincoln -for instance, that Jesus was married and had childrenthey aren't. There is no mention of them anywhere. The reader isn't provided with any evidence -- or, at the very least the sources that are readily accessible to suggest that Jesus may possibly have children. Instead the evidence presented by Lincoln requires the reader to form an unsubstantiated assumption. Although this argument is credible, however it may be, it is without the criteria which are typically required for claims in book.

In fact, when he was speaking several years afterward, Henry Lincoln tells a story of how he and fellow writers came to the conclusion that the lineage of Jesus could have been connected to the Merovingian rulers. While a historian could have looked for clues found in various documents, the tale Lincoln is telling seems to be more like the writers department on the writing department of an American TV show. While the writers sit around discussing the topic, Lincoln remembers it being like a penny just fell. It was almost out from the blue, while the team was discussing why they thought there was something odd regarding the Merovingian line and the information pieces were all in alignment. Merovingian kings. Fishy. Fish are linked to the early Christians. Fish were believed to be a emblem of Jesus. Fish. Jesus. Merovingian. They all must be linked. Then, Lincoln suggests, it was just a matter of putting all the pieces together. When you conduct historical research this way it's clear the reason The Holy Blood and the Holy Grail ultimately received critiques for how that it was written.

What do we go from here? We could consider The Holy Blood and the Holy Grail as the major pivotal moment in the history of the Priory of Sion and how its existence was made public to the general public. We must also acknowledge that the manner the book was written did not align with the standards we expect from non-fiction historical books that make wide-ranging and world-changing assertions. In any case this increases the level of scrutiny we need to give the authors. But does it alter the way we look at our view of the Priory of Sion itself? If they were pushing the limits with their research, are we required to examine the actual society? Next chapter we'll begin to dissect the history of the Priory of Sion and how it has affected the world.

Chapter 4: A Revolt Growing

Although first critiques (and numbers of sale) of The Holy Blood and the Holy Grail were good, it didn't take long before some readers began to see the flaws in the theories. The people who had paid greater focus while the book, or who already had knowledge in the field (or perhaps even understood the way academic research is usually conducted) began to express their reservations about the concept of the book Baigent, Lincoln, and Leigh were putting together. The list of critiques started to increase and. A lot of the criticisms were insignificant, but they were grouped together to create a sort that created a snowball. As the critiques mounted they were confronted with the need to defend themselves as well as to defend the validity in Sion's Priory. Priory of Sion.

If we want looking to analyze the fundamental mistakes in the book's argument It might be helpful to start with the most obvious part which is the thesis. It is believed it is the idea that the bloodline that carries Jesus Christ was preserved in the Merovingian monarchy as well as their descendants. The concept, although seems plausible, it is restricted in its scope due to its nature. One of the biggest issues is the period of time between the emergence of the French Dynasty and the supposed date when Jesus Christ was executed. It is estimated that there are 400 years between the two events, which is enough time for 12 or 13 generations to be alive, dead, and then passed onto their genes. If we think according to the authors of the book aren't we able to conclude that generational generations produced many children at a time? Does it not seem likely that instead of an unifying bloodline, there's an enormous family tree? If these theories are believed as true, there could be more than a one Merovingian family, but also thousands (if there were not thousands) of possible descendents of Christ. If this is the case the modern world could be full of people who (perhaps not knowing it) were all of the same ancestral lineage. The possible progenitors of Jesus could now be in the thousands. It is odd to think that Sion's Priory of Sion would exist to safeguard just one person from such a vast family. It's also impossible that a secret society could be able to keep track of any potential descendant.

It is enough to take a look at the royal palaces of Europe for evidence of this concept in action. The Queen Elizabeth II of England, for instance, can trace her family's roots back centuries. Despite the massive amount of intermarrying and inbreeding that defined the blue bloodlines in the Old World, the current Queen of England shares her heritage with a multitude of other people. Some of them aren't considered to be royalty. With the coups, revolutions, wars, successions and abdications that have been witnessed throughout European time, there is always a possibility that someone is poised to become the next ruler. The notion that there may be only one live descendant from Jesus Christ (who is guarded by the Priory of Sion) seems like a joke when we step away from the text for a second.

This brings us back to Pierre Plantard. Plantard has a special place in this tale, given the fact that The Holy Blood and the Holy Grail specifically names him as the living successor of Jesus Christ. This is an enormous mantle that can be put on one. Also, the fact that they describe him as the current Great Master of the Priory of Sion adds another string to Plantard's already busy bow. What was Plantard himself think? In spite of the assertions that were made by the writers of this bestselling novel, Pierre Plantard has never ever stated that he was possibly a relative of Jesus Christ. Although it is the case that he believes that the lineage of his ancestors can be traced all the way back to Dagobert II (the final of the Merovingian Kings) however, Plantard has stayed away from any claims regarding his family. These claims were included within The Holy Blood and the Holy Grail. In fact, in 1982, Plantard had gone to great lengths to defy the theories outlined in the book and remove himself from any knowledge or position the authors could have imposed on him.

Another issue in the book's critiques is the idea that"the" Holy Grail itself. The idea, as seen at the books on history appears to not exist prior to the 12th century. According to current research numerous scholars of early French literature have claimed that Chretien de Troyes for inventing the concept. The French poet was under the direction of the count Philip who was the ruler of Flanders and was the author of romantic tales of knights. These tales of chivalry were incredibly popular at the time, with oneThe Story of the Grail The Story of the Grail was an enormously popular poem. Like all the popular poems of the time it was copied, borrowed then reworked, revised, and retold in a number of ways. The historian Richard Barber has gone as even as to claim that prior to the year 1180, nobody could have had any idea of what the Holy Grail might have been actually. In addition, Barber comments that the "Sang Real" explanation given in The Holy Blood and the Holy Grail is just an error resulting from the mistranslation made by an English author of the French text, which was written during the fifteenth century. Although it isn't a conclusive evidence, the error appears to be a real result of an era prior to printing presses, in which the production of all books was by hand.

The entire story of the priest which is the most important part of the retelling of

Henry Lincoln is a bit ambiguous. Berenger Sauniere, chief priest of the church in Rennes-le-Chateau was believed to have mysteriously accumulated immense wealth, a phenomenon that the author attributes to his finding out information about the family lineage from Jesus and the secrets of the Priory of Sion. However, we do have the records of the church that Sauniere was a part of. While he was able to fund improvements to the church however, we are aware that this was done through the sale of masses which was a common method to raise money for churches in the past. From 1896 until 1905, the clergy announced sales of the services in local newspapers. Customers could pay with a post-order and receive an acknowledgement during the mass (a benefit when they eventually went to heaven and were evaluated before the gates of heaven.) The business was so popular that the priest was getting more than 150 orders for postal services per day, and the orders did not come from just small religious groups, but also from individuals who were not from France. However, despite all this success, Sauniere himself was far from being a millionaire. There are evidence of the priest seeking a loan from the bank in 1913, and the documents putting his personal finances at only thirteen thousand dollars. If he'd uncovered something that was threatening the basis of the Catholic Church and the Church of Rome, it was also incredibly untrained in how to use blackmail.

The hotel in Rennes-le-Chateau One of the claims in The Holy Blood and the Holy Grail is a blatant lie. The book claims that Berenger Sauniere uncovered an pillar of the cathedral was hollow. It goes as further as to suggest that the one was constructed in the Visigoth style and was connected artistically to that of the Merovingian dynasty. Inside this hollow pillar it is claimed by the authors that the priest discovered a few of parchments hidden. However, this pillar is still within the church. Anyone who visits the church will see it's not hollow. As with every other pillar of the structure, it is solid. There aren't any hidden compartments.

Another error in the artwork of The Holy Blood and the Holy Grail is the depiction of the tomb by the French artist Poussin. Lincoln recalls being informed by his inquiry that the tomb had an uncanny resemblance real-life replica. It's true. What tomb was the first However, it is the fact that Lincoln was completely wrong. The tomb, close to Rennes the place that Lincoln was pointing his finger at wasn't an era of centuries. It was constructed in 1903 and was owned by one of the wives of landowner in the area. Poussin's painting was finished around 250 years before the date of completion. You can go through the text line-by-line and identify the numerous errors that are made in this way. By pointing out the first few but it can be a good way to demonstrate how much research is held to close scrutiny.

Chapter 5: The Truth

Even as the story is unraveling it is helpful to pay a greater amount focus on the situation that was Pierre Plantard. Contrary to the other errors made in the course of research for the novel, Plantard was the one person named directly (and was present to take on the focus.) If, as is suggested in the book Plantard was the alleged descendants to Jesus Christ, how would the implications of this be for his life? One thing it definitely resulted in was forcing people to consider the man's life story and his past, something he might or not have desired.

One of the things discovered through an investigation into the alleged final of the Merovingian line was related with one of most difficult periods in the history of France's recent. In the last years during 1940 France was surrounded by Nazi Germany. The invaders wanted to establish the foundation of a government in France and to establish a government that they controlled and over which they could govern the nation. The government was referred to as the Vichy government due to the place where its headquarters were and was led by an individual named Marshal Petain. Then, one day Petain was approached by a person who signed the name of Varran de Varestra. The letter was a request for Petain to join France to stop any further conflict. Instead of asking for closure to the war However, the sender of this letter referenced "Masonic as well as Jewish" conspiracy members as being the greatest threat to France as well as the rest of the world. The letter's author said he was carrying "about 100 reliable people" to his side that were "devoted for our cause." In the event that Marshal Petain issued the instruction, Varran de Varestra and his trusted men were willing to fight the plot.

The letter appeared to create some controversy within the halls of Vichy government. An investigation was conducted , and the report was prepared upon the request of The Secretary of State was for Interior. Based on the report the so-called "Varran De Varestra was not a different person than Pierre Athanase Marie Plantard, who was born in Paris on the 18th day of Marchin 1920. He was classified as a bachelor and was the child of French parents who had one parent, a butler who died during a work accident. When the letter was composed, Plantard was living with his mother in a 2 bedroom apartment and was living on money he received from his mother's pension.

Pierre Plantard, it seemed was a man with a long-standing time in various organisations. He was the founder and leader of various groups, some of which had an overwhelmingly anti-Semitic or anti-Masonic bent. La Renovation Nationale Francaise, Plantard's current group was described by an police officer who was in charge of the investigation as "purely an idea born from the imagination of Plantard." Although the leader claimed there were 3,245 membersin the group, the actual number was four. In the report, it went on identify Plantard as "one of those sexy pretentious youngsters" who had created and ran fake groups like the ones mentioned above "in attempt to appear significant." This report is highly critical.

So Plantard was a mystery for several years. Plantard reappears in government documents in the year 1954, in which it is revealed that he was in detention in Germany when it was discovered that he had attempted to arrange the gathering of an underground society. The post-war administration in Germany did not like this kind of thing and so detained Plantard until they realized that he posed very little risk to anyone. Plantard was again mentioned in the police files in 1956, but this time in his home country of France. In this instance, the mayor of Annemasse which is an town located in Haute-Savoie in which Plantard was now livingtalked about the arrest for the man named Pierre Plantard in 1953, informing him that he had been indicted for "offences that harmed property." But it's in 1956, also in the town of Annemasse where we discover an extremely significant elements of evidence found in the entire book. In the summer of the year, a man whose name was Pierre Plantard went to the office of the government and registered a new group. He claimed to be one of the founding members who were tasked with "the protection of rights as well as liberties of housing at a low cost." He chose the name to picked for the group is the Priory of

Sion. After this abrupt entry into the history of the federal government Plantard as well as the Priory disappear from the radar.

At this point it is crucial to introduce a new player. Noel Corbu comes to us in the early months of 1956, following several articles on Corbu began appearing in the French media. In that time we can tell that he was not just an owner of a restaurant in Rennes-le-Chateau and was also the proprietor and manager of the home in the name of Berenger Sauniere. The hotel he owned, Hotel de la Tour was situated in a remote location and people were able to see his appearances in newspaper as an attempt to generate publicity and get guests to visit. The hotel had been operating for a long time and it was evident that the principal strategy of marketing was to tell the public about a dark history that was full of treasure and conspiracy theories. You only have to take a look at the headlines in an interview with Corbu interview to understand what the owner was trying to sell. It said 'the Billionaire Priest of Rennes-leChateau's Fabulous Discovery.'

We aren't sure of the precise specifics of what transpired next in the tale, but it's clear that in the the subsequent five years Plantard went to Corbu's home in order to talk with him. Plantard was intrigued by the tale of Berenger Sauniere, and his extraordinary fortune. It was a story that had captured Plantard and he wanted learn more. While it could be true that he was intrigued by the narrative aspect of the story however, it's most likely that he was aware of the potential for financial gain in the story. For someone who had dreams of creating an enviable place in the world this was a fantastic chance. So, after having a conversation Corbu Corbu, Plantard began to create an autobiography. This book loosely took on the tale about Berenger Sauniere along with the church in Rennes-le-Chateau but it also included several important additions. Particulars like the obscure documents that were hidden within the Visigoth pillar were completely Plantard's invention. He even went as that he made the documents created. A man called Phillipe De Cherisey (described as"a "boozy but brilliant Aristocrat") made up the documents which were said to have been stolen from the cathedral. However, the group didn't stop at that point. They also produced two sets of documents, and then deposited them in the National Library of France in an undercover operation. If the story of Plantard were to be doubted, he'd created the evidence that proved his story.

The main issue is that Plantard was not a great writer. He had written an account of the mystery of Rennes-le-Chateau , and he gave it to various publishers. However, no one was interested. Therefore, Plantard decided to turn to one of his acquaintances who was an author who was named Gerard de Sede. De Sede took the book Plantard was working on, cleaned the book, and finally got it published in1967. When we review the specifics of the contract with the publisher we can see some interesting details. Philippe de Cherisey, for example, is listed as having part of the profits. We also have a set of letters which were exchanged among De Cherisey, Plantard, and De Sede which discuss how their elaborate hoax was developing and the many strategies they came up with in case someone would claim that they were lying. One strategy was to use an organisation Plantard had registered before in that of the Priory of Sion, and provide evidence of its long background at the National Library. The item sat for a long time, undiscovered until an inquisitive hands pulled it off the shelf and utilized it to establish its existence. Priory. This curious hand belonged to Henry Lincoln.

It was only a few months following the publication of The Holy Blood and the Holy Grail that the whole of this was made known to the general public. The journalist Jean Luc Chaumeil, writing in 1983, lived in the shadows of the group of people who were so determined to make up the fake. He had personal connections to them and even had a conversation with them. He had not just a set of letters detailing the scheme and the details of the forgery, but also a 44-page confession that was written by Philippe de Cherisey which outlines the way in which the forgery was dealt with. When Chaumeil made his allegations of the group additional researchers like Robert Richardson, Paul Smith along with Henry

Cran (a producer for the BBC) began looking at the tales that were told by Henry Lincoln and his fellow writers. It was Henry Cran who was researching the theories outlined within The Chronicle Chronicle films, that began investigations into the Priory of Sion and its authenticity. The results of his investigation formed the basis of an episode in 1996 of Timewatch entitled The History of a Mystery, in which he was able trace the genealogy that belonged to the Plantard family as early to the sixteenth Century. He realized that instead of being a royal dethroned Plantard's father was actually an artisanal walnut farmer.

Then the truth becomes apparent. It was an elaborate hoax. It was a conspiracy. A scheme to fool the public. Pierre Plantard, far from being the only one to descend from the bloodline from Jesus Christ, was a gambler looking to become famous himself. He was unaware that a small group that included writers and journalists from England could be beguiled by his games particularly to the extent the extent to which they. What started out as a flimsy ploymaybe even an attempt to get the business of a struggling hotel was transformed into an international phenomenon. The release of The Holy Blood and the Holy Grail changed everything. It caused a greater examination of Plantard's tale, which slid under the weight of an investigation.

It was later discovered that the lengthy sequence of family names as well as genealogies which were presented as proof were actually copied of other records. They were tinkered with every now and then, adapted to look more appropriate, while some were just travelogues that were repurposed to suit the particular situation. We know the reasons that prompted those who wrote their tales. De Cherisey states his interest in surrealism. He also was a pioneer in experimental fiction, which included being a part of the 1960s' organization known as The Workshop for Potential Literature, that saw its members create puzzles and codes, ciphers, and tricks on a daily schedule. Plantard like it should be evident by now was desperate to be noticed and had always believed in the creation of secret societies that were mysterious as a way to achieve this end. A lot of the other members such as Gerard de Sede and Noel Corbu for instancewere simply hoping to earn some cash and didn't anticipate that Plantard's idea would become so popular like it did.

The scene must be a bit jarring to observe the men in the group in the midst of trying to give Henry Lincoln more and more details. Lincoln appeared to be genuine in his interest believing in the real extent of the plot that he was getting closer to unraveling. In this respect Lincoln was a master of his game. French agents played his well. They were always available to offer a push towards the right direction or an indication of the best place to look for an answer. In many ways they let Lincoln to be a part of the plot, becoming part of the legacy that was left by The Priory of Sion in much similar ways to how people who read The Holy Blood and the Holy Grail were enticed by the novel. The experience must be shocking to the original writers to realize that they had not only successfully manipulated Lincoln into making the film about their idea however, they also successfully dragged him along for another 10 years, in which he made two films more and recruited his other investigators.

In the late nineties, just after the release of the bestseller, Plantard seemed unable to continue to develop his ideas. In this period Plantard's true character was revealed instead of his created persona of the descended from Jesus Christ. This led to an admission, under an oath in an French courtroom -in which Plantard had invented every aspect of his life. The whole business was, as he acknowledged, just a scam.

His demise in 2000 was not received with a sense of resentment or ridicule in the way one would expect as a fraudster with a huge ego. Also, he was not was mourned as the last of an eminent bloodline. Instead, his passing was greeted with nostalgia. France was left with a cheerful and generally harmless con man. At this point nobody was who believed his story and the whole incident was considered to be an amusing incident. It was a great job, they were thinking, in attempting to fool people. English writers. This was a hilarious story indeed. However, while the majority of

France was able to recognize Plantard for who he actually was however, there were some individuals who remained in the notion that he'd been lying. They held to Sion's Priory of Sion. They included Michael Baigent, Richard Leigh and Dan Brown. Because of their steadfast conviction that the story of Sion Priory Priory of Sion is far from being finished.

Chapter 6: A Victim Of The Priory

In the present it appears that it is true that there exists a plot involving Sion's Priory. Priory of Sion. It's just that it's a completely different one from that we sought to discover. In the first chapter of the book we set out with the idea of revealing an ancient secret that surrounded the very foundational principles of the world's most popular religion. As we go through the tale further and further backwards through time, it becomes evident that the initial idea is based on weak foundations. In spite of the claims of factual accuracy which are repeated throughout works like The Da Vinci Code and The Holy Blood and the Holy Grail We can be certain that this whole story is an attempt to cover up the falsehoods in people's heads. In contrast to a narrative that starts around 0 BC Our tale really begins in the year 1950 AD and attempts to be written into historical records. Although we initially set out to find the perpetrators of a long-running Catholic conspiracy, we need to be asking ourselves: Who were one of the targets of this recent attempt to deceive?

One of the most prominent victims The most obvious victim is Henry Lincoln. We are certain of this -- even at the very least in 1969 when Lincoln first made his first trip on holiday in the south of France -- he sincerely believed in the authenticity of the story that he started to discover. In 2004 he was discussing Pierre Plantard with an interviewer. In his conversation, Lincoln mentioned that the currently deceased Plantard would have been an excellent player. With increasing force, Lincoln passes over the Frenchman's difficulty in reading and points out that the public are actually unaware of Pierre Plantard, much in the same way as we have no idea about Berenger Sauniere. Additionally, he declared, we have no idea of The Priory of Sion. In reality, he said saying that we do not know much about it. Lincoln in the last part portion of his interview complains about the lack of "demonstrable facts," as he calls them. Lincoln admits that the majority of his writing is in reality "hearsay evidence, guesswork , and interpretation." In fact, as Lincoln admits, none his written works on the subject -- not even his own any sort of validity.

It's a flims declaration. It is both an admission and a beacon of optimism. Although he acknowledges having his book is filled with a lot in speculation, the deficiency of evidence to support the history to Plantard (and his Priory of Sion) seems to indicate that there might be something in the book. If we just look a bit deeper or look a bit more perhaps we could find the evidence for that Priory of Sion that men like Henry Lincoln have been searching for for many years.

As scathing as Lincoln's interview may be, it's false. It's not true to say that we don't know anything regarding Plantard and Berenger Sauniere or -- in the case of extension -regarding Sion's Priory. Priory of Sion. Actually, we have a lot of knowledge. One of the most widely-known facts that we have in our collection is regarding the truth about Sion. Priory of Sion is a falsehood. It's a fraud. A scam. A scam, that tricked Lincoln completely. Henry Lincoln was perhaps the first victim of this scam and this was such a huge scam that it seems to be enduring to this day. In the back of Henry Lincoln's head is the constant idea that there could be an actual Priory of Sion after all. The idea nags at Lincoln and is unable to permit Lincoln to deny the idea completely.

We know it is true that there was evidence that the Priory of Sion was indeed an elaborate plot by a few French conmen, we recognize that the first victims were the ones who helped to make the lie more popular. This brings our to the second step of the process, and one of the most crucial concerns of them all. Did the authors of The Holy Blood and the Holy Grail simply the victims of an elaborate fraud? Did they consent to be fooled? Was it possible that they were part of the scheme?

For more details on this topic, it might be beneficial to look up one of the authors who actually exposed the truth behind Plantard as well as the Priory of Sion. Jean Luc Chaumeil released his own book in 1979. It was just a few months following the airing of the final movie in the trilogy that Henry Lincoln produced for Chronicle. It took three years prior to the publication of the book written by Henry Lincoln, Richard Leigh

Richard Leigh, and Michael Baigent, at a period when these three men were believed to be conducting (supposedly) meticulous research. In an interview later on Channel Four television (a British broadcaster), Chaumeil mentions a story of his efforts to connect with the authors of The Holy Blood and the Holy Grail. Chaumeil insists that he tried to get in touch with the trio for up to an entire year before the publication date to inform readers to the nature and extent of the fraud.

The allegations would have a significant impact on our perception of the writers of The Holy Blood and the Holy Grail. If they deliberately ignored an instruction and released their thoughts anyway and without a thorough check through Chaumeil's remarks which would make their decision-making process suspect at the very least. The accusation was directed at Michael Baigent himself during the filming of an investigation by actor and TV historian Tony Blackburn. If asked if the French journalist's allegations were true, Baigent states that he is unable to remember the event. Not only that, but Baigent also states the Chaumeil's position was that he "never likely to be near to the inner circles that comprised the Priory." It's unclear who Baigent refers to in his statement. This could be an allusion to the men who created the Priory and had forged the documents that successfully deceived people. It could refer to the real Priory of Sion themselves.

However, Tony Robinson followed up the question by asking Baigent what his thoughts were regarding Chaumeil's claims that the whole Priory of Sion organization was just an absurdist dream. Baigent's response is straightforward and direct. "He's not right," Baigent exclaims. When asked to be certain that the journalist's account is wrong, Baigent puts forward his personal research abilities and skills to prove it. He has read the documents on his own, Baigent tells his interviewer that he has studied them, for six years, and has spent the time looking over and studying Sion's Priory. Priory of Sion. To this extent and with all his research done, Baigent states that he is "satisfied that the Priory exists." It's difficult to Baigent to make any more clear about his beliefs. In the present Baigent seems to be to be convinced of the fact that the documents and the histories were presented before the public in The Holy Blood and the Holy Grail were entirely legitimate.

In reality, Baigent has gone on repeatedly and repeatedly stated that the team he was with reviewed, scrutinized and verified every piece of details they came across in their investigation. Baigent does not only Baigent affirm that he and his team examined every possibility and were satisfied with the results, claiming that it "proved true." The manner and thoroughness of the checking isn't mentioned, however, it's impossible to say that it would be considered to have been completely complete. In 1993, everyone who was involved in the French aspect of the fraud was able to admit their guilt. The documents -- which included Dossiers Secrets, which were among the Dossiers Secrets that had been kept in the National Library of France -were confirmed to be fakes.

But Baigent did not relent. He remained firm. Holy Blood and the Holy Grail was reprinted in the year 1996 and Baigent took time to respond to these allegations in a post-word he created specifically in the context of the latest edition. Together with others who wrote the text it was suggested that the allegations made on the work and the theories it defended were on the shaky foundations. Baigent, Leigh, and Lincoln claimed that Plantard was not able for "gain financial gain or any other benefit" by fabricating documents. They repeated that they believed that there were no grounds to believe Plantard's claims. It's a stretch to believe that the authors can truly be convinced they were right that Leonardo da Vinci and Sir Isaac Newton had led hidden lives and kept secret the lineage of Jesus Christ, but not that Pierre Plantard could have invented or even lied concerning Sion's Priory. Priory of Sion.

It is the roots of the Priory which have triggered some of the most vocal defenses by the writers of The Holy Blood and the Holy Grail. In the follow-up to their most popular book called The Messianic Legacy, the authors reaffirmed their conviction that there is The Priory of Sion. Although the book was released in 1987, a long time after the Chaumeil articles exposed that the facts were true, Baigent, Leigh, and Lincoln confirmed their belief that the Priory's existence was real. In addition, the sequel clarified exactly what they believed about the claims that their prior assertions may not have been accurate. In one chapter in the novel, they admit that "nothing seemed straightforward" while researching the Priory. They provide a detailed description of the character of the Priory of Sion in which they examine its history in relation to "a Holographic image." The image, they claim was altered, moved around and changed its appearance in different lighting. From one perspective according to the book, it appears that the Priory of Sion was believed as an "influential wealthy and powerful world-wide secret society" however, they acknowledge that, in a different perspective it appears that the Priory could be simply an "dazzlingly imaginative hoax created by a few individuals with no intention of pursuing themselves." Maybe, the authors assert that both were correct.

This is a clever strategy employed by the writers. When they write this piece they put their own view of the hoax onto the same level as the truth. Both versions are the same however, they suggest, only different perspectives. However, while the notion of it was the Priory of Sion is nothing more than a scam was supported by an abundance of proof and confessions their claims regarding the real nature of the Priory were still made based on documents recognized as fraudulent. Although it may appear that the authors were sensible in introducing some doubt, their acceptance of anything but. Again, they resort to relying on their poor research abilities that are wrapped in persuasive rhetoric.

It is enough to look over Baigent's history to gain some information about why he might be inclined to be a part of Sion's Priory of Sion. Baigent's personal story indicates that he is likely to be influenced by the notion that there is an agenda that is negative within the Catholic Church. Based on his own memories, Baigent was raised in a fervently Catholic family. The entirety of his childhood was marked by commitment to the church, and the possibility of any disaffection of their doctrines could be an expression of resentment against the establishment. In his hometown in New Zealand, Michael Baigent and his family were known to attend the community Catholic Church at least three times per week. At the age of five, he even offered private lessons by an instructor in theology on the doctrine and history that governed the Catholic Church. As with most teens, he resisted his parents and the underlying institutional structures in his daily life. However, while many teenagers resort to alcohol or drugs however, younger Michael Baigent still felt the desire to scratch that religious scratch. In the course of a few months that lasted, he attended every kind of church that could. The Anglicans The Anglicans, the Methodists as well as the Presbyterians along with the Mormons all invited him to their church. However, he was unable to find his answers that he had been searching for.

After that, while going out to study at a university Michael Baigent changed his field of research. Although he was originally accepted to an academic degree in science but he decided to change classes and study comparative religion. Maybe if he'd stuck to the original program, he could have gained a greater understanding of how to get tangible results from research. However, his interest while at the university started to become more mysterious. Along with the classes on comparative religions He began to expand his interests to more obscure aspects of theology. He was a part of a group called The Builders of Adytum which were a group that practiced the largely unexplored practice known as Christian Kabbalah. Through his college years He was interested in the more obscure areas in his Christian world, which was a far cry from the traditional Roman Catholic upbringing.

In the end, this route brought him eventually to England. When he moved towards London in the 70s, the flat he rented with an individual named Richard Leigh. They became close friends , and soon realized an affinity for the odd elements of the religion. In the meantime, Baigent was pursuing a somewhat successful career as a journalist. But after Richard Leigh introduced Baigent to the man who was Henry Lincoln, he was eager to end his career. When Lincoln expressed his desire to be a part of the documentary he was creating to be broadcast by BBC, BBC, Baigent quickly sold all of his equipment for photography to finance his research along with the duo of writers. Baigent even began working shifts during the night for a soft drink manufacturing facility to earn a living as he conducted the initial study of what would later be The Holy Blood and the Holy Grail. It's possible to conclude at this point Michael Baigent was heavily invested in the existence of the Priory of Sion and was interested in possible evidence that suggested there could be a deeper meaning to this Catholic doctrine. The research conducted by the team gave him an ideal reason to justify his growing disbelief of organized religion, and also a way to indulge in his interest in the mysteries of the practice. Baigent admits to this when he testifies in the courtroom that "with retrospectively, I've been obsessed with the Priory of Sion]."

In the years following the publication of The Holy Blood and the Holy Grail, Michael Baigent was evidently still in his fascination. A man whose name is Paul Smith, a noted skeptical of the theories presented in the novel, was able to see Baigent during 1993. While Smith claims that Baigent was friendly and polite, he was amazed to discover Baigent's insistence regarding his belief in the Priory of Sion, that the Merovingian bloodline could easily be traced back to the present as well as it was believed that there was a Line of David (and thus Jesus Christ) was a possible fact. In the documents and papers that Baigent kept in his house, Smith discovered various sources that appeared to establish that the legend that was told about Sauniere along with the church in Rennes-le-Chateau was not a true story. They were either ignored or ignored. According Smith Smith the eminent evidences were at the feet of a person whom "did have no idea how use themcorrectly." Baigent, Smith claims preferred exploring "non-sequiturs that were related to"pseudo-history."

The more we know the more we know about Michael Baigent, the more it is possible to connect with his character. While he could be proven to be wrong repeatedly but there is nothing shady to his belief that there is a Priory of Sion. It is more likely that he will be someone who is able to think differently when confronted by evidence that is in opposition to his perception. This isn't to say that he doesn't look into evidence. When it comes to the process of his investigation to write The Holy Blood and the Holy Grail, Baigent and his co-authors analyzed the vast amount of evidence throughout many years. The problem is the method of analysis Baigent and his co-authors could adopt. Each time they analyzed the source, they were content to only use information that confirmed their views, and reject anything that could cause them to reconsider their beliefs. Confessions and conspiracy theories from people like Pierre Plantard were readily dismissed due to the fact that Baigent and his co-writers considered the concept that there was a Priory of Sion with an almost religious fervor. They believed in the concept regardless of the evidence that was in opposition.

An anecdote may provide some insight into the issue. The former editor for the Spectator, Matthew d'Ancona recalls an informal luncheon that was held in the late 1990s at an eatery in central London known as L'Amico. The event was divided into two distinct'sides. On one hand was a small group right-of-center political thinkers whose main shared ideology was to disengage Britain away from European Union. On the other hand, there was the group that D'Ancona called'men who don't go out often. They included Michael Baigent and Richard Leigh. The gathering was created by the two authors with an intention of investigating members of the Eurosceptic group for any information. D'Ancona recalls the questions being asked whether the right-wingers have encountered anything unusual in their quest to disengage Britain and the EU? Did they ever have the notion that there might be a hidden motive behind the birth and development of the European Union? Could it be thatinstead of creating an international federation for purposes of governance and trade—there could be a plot to accomplish something as bizarre as restoring the bloodline that was established by Jesus Christ to a position of power maybe? According to D'Ancona The authors of The Holy Blood and the Holy Grail put together the luncheon with the intent of reaffirming one their most bizarre concepts. This speaks volumes about the lengths they went to prove their point. It's odd to see this as the work of people who are aware of the utterly false nature of their own opinions.

It is evident that there is a believable belief among the authors of The Holy Blood and the Holy Grail that the Priory of Sion is actually a reality. Certain Michael Baigent and Richard Leigh believe in the proof they have seen up to the point where they would stand up for themselves on an oath. The very principles that underlie their suit against Dan Brown seem to suggest that it was the idea that their theories might be faulty that led to the problem and not the actual plagiarism. However, there was one person who was not present at the trial. It is difficult to determine the convictions that shaped Henry Lincoln seems a bit more difficult.

Many believe the possibility that Henry Lincoln was much quicker to grasp the truth of The Priory story. After being an author in the fields of television and film for a number of decades, Lincoln was aware of the skills needed to write a story and convey it effectively. It could be that when he saw the amount of profits that were to be earned from creating The Holy Blood and the Holy Grail He saw it as no different from writing another story for Doctor Who or some other science fiction B-movie. Lincoln was one of those who had established a successful television career on the basis of a small deceit. He wasn't an archaeologist or historian but was pleased to be portrayed as an archaeologist on Chronicle and other shows on TV. What made participating in the plot behind Sion's Priory Priory of Sion any different than trying to appear as a historian? It is evident that it was not the the end all of Henry Lincoln.

Since The Holy Blood and the Holy Grail was releasedand particularly after The Da Vinci Code's popularity --- Henry Lincoln has given many interviews. One of them offered a glimpse into how he sees the evidence supporting that there was a Priory of Sion. In the course of the conversation, Lincoln quite freely admits that the documents -like Dossiers Secrets Dossiers Secrets -- are evidence for "absolutely nothing" other than the fact that they were created. The same, he claims, is true for all documents. Lincoln concludes the abstract notion by saying that "nothing is superior to everything else."

"In the world of history," he suggests, "nothing is true, so there's nothing to get caught on." This is an insightful admission of the way Lincoln regards his work in the book of history. It reveals how different his criteria of proof differ different from those of the average historian and how he regards his work as more like an essay than an academic piece. In fact, the remarks made by Henry Lincoln seem to place him on the same level with Dan Brown. The reason perhaps Lincoln was not in attendance in

The Da Vinci Code trial was because he was able to see more of him as Dan Brown. To critique Brown would be admitting that the fact that he was not right. Although he might have believed that there was a Priory of Sion at the time of his writing however, it appears that Lincoln is the only one of the authors who have realized the nature of the institution.

Chapter 7: The Fallout

Through the course of this book, it's become ever more apparent that any claims about whether there was a Priory of Sion is fundamentally incorrect. But this hasn't prevented a variety of publications including brochures, books and films, articles or television programs, as well as other media from blaring over the theories that are presented within The Holy Blood and the Holy Grail. Even after The French conspiracy has proved that these theories are false many have taken on these ideas and carried the myths. Today, there are many media outlets that claim that they can inform people of the truth of the myth. In spite of the evidence that has been presented in the past, what do people consider regarding what is known about the Priory of Sion today?

As one would expect There are a myriad of different theories about the essence of Sion's Priory. An easy Google search can yield more than 360,000 results for the search term "Priory of Sion. It has its own dedicated website, Wikipedia pages, and YouTube videos that claim to provide the public with the most accurate explanation of what the society actually is. In addition, Google will make some suggestions for the avid user and will mention Knights Templar, Mary Magdalen, Opus Dei, and the Illuminati as being searches closely related with Sion. Priory of Sion. It is easy to determine which kind of company search terms represent.

If you've spent a an extensive amount of time perusing the information that is online there are a lot of themes and concepts that are repeated. While you browse pages after webpage they will pop over and over. Some of them haven't been addressed in the text, but are now considered crucial to the current understanding of the Priory of Sion. Therefore, let's spend some time following some of these tangents in order to better comprehend how the Priory of Sion means in the current Internet age.

Mary Magdalena

Mary Magdalen is perhaps one of the most important characters in the tale, one we've not even touched on in the course of the book. Mary Magdalen is a key character in the tale about The Priory of Sion, and one that goes far beyond the the issues of deceit and fraud which are the basis of many of the other themes in this book. Although her name is well-known all over the globe, there's an enormous amount of misinformation regarding who exactly Mary Magdalen really was and what she was doing with respect to the biblical Jesus Christ. Jesus Christ. The story of Mary Magdalen is characterized by violent attack on her character and could be one of the first instances of misrepresentation and slander. Who did Mary Magdalen really represent?

The confusion regarding Mary Magdalen's identity is due to being aware that she is a relative of the much more famous biblical character. In no way is she a duplicate of Mary Magdalen, the mother of Jesus - the Virgin Mary also known as Mary of Bethany who had the status of being the sibling of Lazarus Mary Magdalen plays an odd role in the tale in that of the New Testament. Much like the apostles she was believed to have traveled with Jesus and appears in numerous tales of Jesus, the Jesus, the son of God. One of them is the account of his death, in which she witness the crucifixion as well as the resurrection from afar. In all four gospels, she is mentioned 12 times. Although it may seem like an insignificant number, it is actually more than many of the less famous disciples.

In the Middle Ages, there was an abrupt change in the manner she was portrayed to the public. Although the Bible seems to portray her as a disciple of Christ but her reputation was stained by the tarnish of her name. In error (according to the majority of experts) Mary Magdalen is depicted as an "repentant prostitute" to the adherents of Western Christianity. This is supported by scant evidence from the original Bible Many clergy, preachers and those belonging to holy order were more than content to call Mary Magdalen an example like the description of a "loose female." Through the decades, she was regarded mostly for her fake history as a prostitute, and not for her faith in Jesus Christ, the Biblical Jesus.

In other words, if Mary didn't deserve this title, what does the Bible really tell us about her? We do know that Jesus expelled seven demons who were in her body. In both gospels Luke as well as Mark (the one in Mark is more detailed on the subject) Mary is mentioned as one who was a follower of Jesus along with the Apostles when they "traveled around from one town and village to the next." The gospels say that it was Jesus as they say as the one who washed Mary from the demons who had been afflicting her, which people have believed to be the cure for mental health issues that weren't well-known in the time.

In the crucifixion where Mary Magdalen is able to play a significant role, but. When Jesus Christ is executed, Mary Magdalen plays a significant role. Jesus Christ, she witnesses three important moments. She was present at the time of the crucifixion as well as at the burial as well as one of the first to notice that the tomb has been empty for a couple of days afterward. The gospels the authors of Mark, Matthew, and John mention her in these instances, naming her and Luke did not mention any names, did mention her presence "women who followed Jesus to Galilee." In this way it is safe to conclude that in any account of the

Bible of Jesus' execution Jesus Christ -- Mary Magdalen was in the scene.

However, she also has an important part. Through Mark, Matthew, and John the role the Mary Magdalen who is the first witness to the most significant of Christian events that is the resurrection. Three gospels mention Mary Magdalen as a single person or with other people as the first person to realize that Christ's tomb Christ was empty. In several passages in Mark and John the author makes it explicit that Mary Magdalen was the first person who the risen Christ was revealed. In some passages, it's explicit that the meeting was an intimate one that is shared by Jesus Mary Magdalen and Jesus Christ which is not a right granted by many highly regarded apostles. This suggests that she has an significant role in the life and ministry of Jesus Christ, especially by the time he's executed.

And not only that, the way she is depicted in the gospels appears to make her an important persona. Every time a group or women are identified in gospels like Mark for instance the gospel of Mark, it's Mary Magdalen who is mentioned first. In all four gospels that are major her name is mentioned in a manner that according to historical scholar Carla Ricci -- "cannot be considered as fortuitous." The mention of her name is intentional and the importance that the authors place on her appearance is evidently deliberate. How did she change from a prominent disciple of Christ to the woman whose name was the word used to describe prostitutes?

We have already established that the notion of Mary Magdalen being prostitute who repents is not in the Gospels. Mary Magdalen is not found anywhere else in the canonical Bible (though she appears in several books that were apparently removed from the list). The sullying of the name of Mary Magdalen in the time of Pope Gregory I. In 591, he made an opinion that conjured Mary Magdalen with an unnamed sinner from the Bible. He fashioned what is referred to as the "composite Mary." This means that she would have a reputation for the sins committed by several other people not listed in the bible text. In time, the seven demons said to be removed from Mary's body through Jesus became the symbol of the seven sins that are considered capital and in time Mary Magdalen began to be accused of being a symbol of covetousness and lust.

There is also a tangled background to Mary Magdalen's story. Alongside her unjust denigration through her own Catholic Church. There are supposed to be numerous other sources dating from when gospels were composed that make her more significant to Christianity. Also known by the name of Gnostic gospels, there exist several books that are not part of the Bible. Although Matthew, Mark, Luke and John are considered to be the four accepted gospels there's stories from other apostles like Philip. In some way or another the gospels were not selected for inclusion in the "official biblical canon. They were reassembled in the present as the Apocrypha and very little of their texts are accessible. Perhaps most important, we've discovered that there was at some point or other -an Gospel that was written by Mary.

The Gospel of Mary differs from other texts in a variety of ways. It gives greater importance to women's roles within the first Christian Church. It is believed that the text was composed during the same time period in The Gospel of Philip (also in the Apocrypha) however, the fragments that we have from the Gospel of Mary originate from three centuries ago. It is generally believed that the Mary in this title was Mary Magdalena. In the the gospels, there is the acknowledgment that Mary was the one who was favored by Jesus in comparison to all his disciples. In addition, Peter confessing that Jesus was a fan of Mary "more than all the other women," Levi suggests that "the Saviour ... loved Mary Magdalen more than we do."

However, there are additional references to Mary from the Apocrypha. The Gospel of Philip the woman is described as using the Greek word that means companion, partner or companion. In various ways, Philip describes how the love displayed towards her by Jesus resulted in anger and jealousy among the other disciples in addition to mentioning that Christ was known to "kiss her frequently." It is these references such as these that are the foundation for one of the most important conceits that is Sion's Priory of Sion.

As we've seen previously in this book The Holy Blood and the Holy Grail is a hard-working book to establish the idea that Jesus had children. According to their theory the theory suggests that it is Mary Magdalen who not only gave birth to the divine bloodline she was also Jesus's wife. The evidence is based on things like the apparent preference that the apostles appear to have given to her throughout the Gospels. They also claim the fact that Jesus appeared at her private times as being the only person Jesus met upon his return to the world and even mentions of within the Gospel of Philip that seem to indicate the relationship between a couple. They claim that it was normal for to a Jewish man living in the Near East at the time to marry and have children, to the point that it wasn't worth being mentioned in the text, unless as a passing reference. Mary Magdalen, they argue is actually Mary, the spouse of Jesus Christ.

This is the point where one of the more suspicious aspects of the novel comes into the spotlight. In The Holy Blood and the Holy Grail (as in The Da Vinci Code) that Mary Magdalen became an enemy of the Catholic Church. We've already discussed the obvious jealousy other disciples were believed to feel toward her and her demonization by the church is thought to be part of the Catholic conspiracy to retain the power. Her reputation was damaged in order to denigrate her, and also to undermine the possibility of bloodline descent from Jesus Christ. Although a descendant from Jesus could be an issue for Jesus's Pope as God's representative on Earth but the child of prostitutes was not given much attention. Campaign against Mary Magdalen wasn't only an attempt to reinforcing patriarchal values through the use of a sacred text but was also an attempt to denigrate the only that could be a threat that could have posed a threat to the Catholic Church's authority. In this respect they were certainly successful.

Did they? In any case, the books like The Holy Blood and the Holy Grail and The Da

Vinci Code have caused a major rethinking of the persona of Mary Magdalena. As we've observed, it is possible to use the internet to seek out more information on topics connected with Sion and the Priory of Sion. If, while you search online, you find the tangents as well as the related theories, they may find a myriad of sources that make the claim regarding the actual nature of Mary Magdalena. Even though she may not be one of the wives of Jesus Christ (and her being connected to Sion's Priory of Sion is yet another aspect of the fake) There are studies and other sources on the internet that examine the reputation and changing perceptions of this person over time. By enticing people to find out more about Mary Magdalen, proving fake works on her and about the Priory of Sion can point readers and viewers to an ounce of truth. In this regard at the very the very least, it appears like this Priory of Sion is retroactively performing a significant role to encourage Mary Magdalen.

Although they may not be safeguarding a fictional bloodline, they're making a difference in encouraging people to look deeper into the real story behind one of the Bible's most mysterious characters. In a way that no one would have expected, works such as The Holy Blood and the Holy Grail have managed to change the public's perception of Mary Magdalen or at the very least, start the process of an examination of the person she really was. In this way, it could even be possible to say this: The Priory of Sion have partly achieved their objective even though they were proved to be a total hoax.

Chapter 8: The Grand Masters Grand Masters

Another important aspect of the legend that surrounds the Priory of Sion is the praise of the alleged Grand Masters. In establishing the background for this Priory, Plantard and his colleagues meticulously compiled the names of those they believed could be members of a secret anti-Catholic group. It even gave this job an official title, naming those who were the Grand Masters as Nautonnier the Old French word that translates roughly to "navigator. In the esoteric world the title Nautonnier is often known in various ways as Grand Master, and that is why it is the title used within both The Da Vinci Code and The Holy Blood and the Holy Grail.

The method by the way that the list of former Grand Masters was put together was among the most obscure elements that was part of the Priory of Sion hoax and it has received the most interest from the general public. With the pseudonym Philippe Toscan du Plantier, Pierre Plantard painstakingly assembled his list that dates from 1188 to the 1960s. The list was published as part of the Dossiers Secrets d'Henri Lobineau, which was the document that he and his team concealed inside the National Library of France and were waiting for others to discover.

The list was a bit complicated when it was created. It is a clear idea that every person on the list and identified by name was dead when Plantard wrote his name on the list. That meant there was no living person who could claim their involvement. If anyone from the family or biographer spoke out and challenged the involvement of a particular individual, Plantard as well as his accomplices could easily base their case on the argument it was because they were the Priory of Sion was a secret society, and that it was unlikely that The Grand Master actually revealing the public about the existence of the Priory.

The list contains many of the most famous writers and artists in European history, but it's not completely lacking a foundation. Actually most of the names included on the list can be listed on the membership list of the Ancient Mystical Order Rosae Crucis which was a different fabricated secret society of religious cults that became increasingly popular in France during the time of Plantard's writing. Additionally to that, many of those who are on the list have been recognized for having a vague fascination with the occult, and their inclusion is a reflection of the notions and beliefs that people already have.

In the interest of It is worth noting that Plantard made an interesting bit of history by writing The Dossiers Secrets. According to Plantard that his Priory of Sion and the Knights Templar shared a common Grand Master for a lengthy period of time. This was until 1188, at which point there was a split. After that, every society had a distinct leader. Plantard even linked this into an actual historical event called The Cutting of the Elm. The cutting was an official event that occurred that occurred between English and French monarchies, which was used to honor the talks that took place between Franks with the Normans. While the English were sitting under an enclave of shade but the French were made to endure the heat from the sun. After the conclusion of the negotiations in the end, the French

King requested that the trees be removed. This was an indication that the English would not be given consideration should they persist in their disagreement. For reasons that were not explicitly made explicit, this historic incident had a profound influence to The Grand Master from Sion's Priory of Sion. These little details are but one way that Plantard tried to give his invention a sense authenticity, giving readers enough information to enable them to make their own conclusion.

The entire list includes 26 men. In order of chronology they are:

* Jean de Gisors
* Marie de Saint-Clair
* Guillaume de Gisors
* Edouard de Bar
* Jeanne de Bar
* Jean de Saint-Clair
* Blanche d'Evreux
* Nicolas Flamel
* Rene d'Anjou
* Iolande de Bar
* Sandro Filipepi
* Leonard da Vinci
* Connetable de Bourbon

* Ferdinand de Gonzague
* Louis de Nevers
* Robert Fludd
* J. Valentin Andrea
* Robert Boyle
* Isaac Newton
* Charles Radclyffe
* Charles de Lorraine
* Maximilian de Lorraine
* Charles Nodier
* Victor Hugo
* Claude Debussy
* and Jean Cocteau

A quick glance through the list will reveal a variety of less well-known and famous individuals. Leonardo da Vinci and Isaac Newton are two names that instantly grab the attention and is surely for which Dan Brown titled his book The Da Vinci Code - but other members like Robert Fludd and Edouard de Bar are not as popular. This is a smart tactic that was employed by the man who created the lists upon which Plantard was able to base his own. By obscuring attention-grabbing names in the midst of less interesting (though legitimate as a whole) terms, the list gives an incredible sense of credibility for the listing. It's a trickery method that is applied to a religious fraud.

However, this isn't all there is to it. There are other documents written by Plantard which expand his listing of Grand Masters. One of them is called Le Cercle d'Ulysse . It was also a fake as well as planted evidence. It says that Francois ducaud-Bourget is the most recent in the long list of Grand Masters. However, Francois Ducaud Bourget was not simply another name. It was actually one of the names given to a person that Plantard had a personal relationship with. He was an Catholic priest, and was known for being traditionalist. Plantard was employed by the man as sexton in his time in the second World War. Plantard identified him as the Grand Master after the death of Jean Cocteau. This is an example of the hoaxer forming the circle around himself. Alongside the assertions Plantard made about having Merovingian roots Plantard was using the personal experiences to provide basis for a complex hoax.

However, it didn't require long for Dossiers Secrets to be exposed as being bogus.

Although there are numerous tests available that determine the date of a specific piece of paper or document (useful in evaluating purportedly old sources) however, none of this was pertinent to Dossiers Secrets. It was running through to today it was not necessary for Plantard to say it was anything else than an actual list from an earlier order. But that didn't mean that it could not be quickly proven to be false. The hoax was traced to Plantard's hands and, once others in the group admitted to this hoax, it didn't take long before the ruse was revealed (at the very least at least in France.) However, in the beginning of the hoax's disclosure, Plantard kept decidedly quiet. He was heavily involved in all aspects of the plot and it should come as not a surprise to anyone to learn the fact that Plantard was able to create an updated List of Grand Masters. In the course of a 1989 rerun on the tale of the Priory of Sion, Plantard presented his updated list to the general public. The first list, as he knew that was not a success, so the second one was a more private event. There are no names like Leonardo da Vinci and Isaac Newton and the new list appears to have more of a French focus. Furthermore, it only tracks back the Grand Masters back to the 1600s, and makes less lofty claims than the previous Dossiers Secrets. In 1993, however the list was proved to be fake.

The famous status of the Grand Masters is one of the most memorable features that is Sion's Priory of Sion. When people try to unravel the mysteries for themselves One of the main areas of interest is the fame of those who were involved. If it's enough to invite in some of the most brilliant thinkers, as the hoax claims that there is some truth to the story. By doing this, the hoax plays with the famous abilities of the members and draws legitimacy from their achievements in order to make Sion's Priory of Sion seem more real.

Although this may be the main draw that is the Priory of Sion (thanks to The Da Vinci Code, it's at least just as well-known as the concept of the existence of a divine bloodline) However, it is quite possible that the listing of Grand Masters attracted far too many eyes. When the institution was nothing more than secret protectors of a conspiracy concept, it was virtually impossible to prove completely. However, the presence of well-known names is another avenue to disprove Plantard's elaborate fraud. Many scholars, researchers and academics have demonstrated the utmost ease that certain people on the list might not have been involved due to factors like geographical place of residence, ideological motivation or the fact being dead when they were in charge of an underground society. In this regard, Plantard seems to have exaggerated in his ambition. The people he was hoping to bring into his Priory of Sion were almost too famous to be good for him.

Chapter 9: 'Circuit Douo'

"De Gaulle is a spokesman for Moscow and is surrounded by a gang of liars connected in and the Jewish Freemason the world of high-end financial institutions'
Jean Garde

"[De Gaulleis in a conscious way taking us to places we don't would like to go, towards Communism. De Gaulle is the Catholic military, aristocratic, and French guarantee of this huge betrayal'
Abbe Georges de Nantes

As we have seen in previous chapters, during the second quarter of the 1950s, Pierre Plantard had aligned himself with, and was a part of, Rightist ideology and politics. In 1956, he established an organization that was a Traditionalist Catholic lay order named the Priory of Sion in an area in eastern France known as Annemasse. The stated goal for the Priory of Sion was to "renew" France by reestablishing an Ancien Regime, a very typical goal for a right-wing Traditionalist organization. In this way, they Priory of Sion immediately became involved in the local political scene of Annemasse and focused its attention on the issue of housing development and construction, which required huge sums of money that were made available for reconstruction after the war. Pierre Plantard subsequently ran to be a candidate for Annemasse's local authority for housing. In the meantime, it was the Priory of Sion published an regular monthly newsletter that was focused on Annemasse politics as well as the issue of housing.

A year and a half following, Plantard 'suddenly' became the primary media representative of The Committees of Public Safety that played a role in the returning in Charles de Gaulle to power during the non-violent French Rightist coup in May 1958. Although some ardent Gaullists like Delbecque may accept Plantard's "position" to be the Committee of Public Safety 'secretary of public relations' during the coup, nobody in or within the de Gaulle team has confirmed Plantard was directly working with de Gaulle or working with his approval. Based on Baigent, Leigh, and Lincoln however, Plantard claimed to them in 1979 that he had been hired in direct contact with de Gaulle:

* When our first encounter with M. Plantard in 1979 we were told by him his story of how Charles de Gaulle had personally wanted him to lead his French Committees of Public Safety and, after their mission of putting the General in his position was complete and he was appointed to head their dissolution.[1] [Baigent Leigh, and Lincoln[Baigent, Leigh and Lincoln]

As will be demonstrated in the near future, Plantard was making such claims the year 1959. What's most interesting about these assertions is that, in the event that they are true, are a complete mockery of the persistent claims of de Gaulle that he was absolutely no involvement in his Rightist coup that brought him back to the power of. If Plantard was directly working for de Gaulle and was his'secretary for propagandism sure the man would have realized that attempting to directly link de Gaulle to the control of Committees of Public Safety would be extremely embarrassing for the President? Was Plantard have been so stupid? Was Plantard actually engaged in subverting de Gaulle through clever use of propaganda? In the preceding section, there was a lot of Rightists who were fervently seeking for the end of the disgraced Fourth Republic but who also were extremely distrustful of de Gaulle due to his previous extreme opposition to his Vichy regime. Thus, even though they were prepared to join with de Gaulle in this coup, they were extremely sceptical regarding the previous General. Most importantly the suspicion and distrust could have been incredibly justified given the way that things unfolded during both the latter half of 1958 , and the following year.

Many of de Gaulle's closest supporters eventually turned against him due to his apparent 'traitorous' attitude regarding the Algerian question, as we have seen in the previous chapter. Even if Plantard was a fervent Gaullist during the year 1958, his devotion to de Gaulle could have been, as it was for a lot of others, severely tested in 1959. As it became apparent that de Gaulle didn't have an intention of remaining in Algeria and he was a an enemy of the public for a number of Rightists and a majority of Ultras. What is the camp that Plantard end up in? It is hoped that the answer will become evident as the study continues!

Like numerous Ultras immediately began painting de Gaulle as a shady Communist and with the additional surprise that he was an instrument of the much-disliked "Jews"! As per Alexander Harrison many Ultras were:

* '...convinced that de Gaulle was "surrounded by more than enough Jews" and that he was a representative to represent Jewish economic interests... (andthe fact the fact that de Gaulle himself "had Jewish blood" [italics added] [2] Alexander Harrison.

A close friend with Jean Ousset, named Jean Gardes even wrote an article that said that de Gaulle was:

* '...an agent from Moscow and surrounded by a cadre of lackeys with connections in an 'insider' of the Jewish Freemason the world of high finance' [italics added[3] Alexander Harrison[Alexander Harrison].

It is important to note the fact that Jean Gardes was actually a Colonel in the French military. His specialty included psychological warfare. It is important to note of the distinctness.

As for the extreme Catholic Right, it was widely believed the de Gaulle campaign was an opportunistic puppet of the Jews and Communists. Abbe Georges de Nantes said that de Gaulle was:

* '...was returned in the hands of great financiers to dismantle...the French Empire"[italics added[4] Abbe Georges de Nantes[Abbe Georges de Nantes].

For "great financiers" look up Jewish bankers! Additionally:

* "De Gaulle's policy was a blessing to his country's Communist bloc: Charles de Gaulle is able to convince people that he's seeking a Centrist position, which is a one that rules everything and is devoid of untruthful compromise, is financially and morally acceptable as well as a guarantee of prosperity in the economy and an easy way to attain peace, at the same time, he is willingly leading us to a place we would never like to go and that is to Communism.

He is Catholic and military, aristocratic and, for nations outside as well as the French the guarantor for this huge betrayal. He is a perfect candidate for this job. the ability to judge coldness with a calculating eye and two qualities that the Gospel acknowledges as characteristics of the sons of devil and the capacity to lie in a way that is outrageous and the capability of murdering or destroying people once they've mastered the game in full. I'll say it again that it could have been much more beneficial for us and, I'm afraid, for this person that has never been born' [italics addedAbbe Georges de Nancy[Abbe Georges de Nantes].

It is evident from the passages above that when he was once"the darling of the right de Gaulle at the end of 1959, was an absolute "Great Betrayer".

Also in 1959, there was a abrupt publication of the Priory of Sion newsletter CIRCUIT following a three-year hiatus. The new editions included no mention of Council Housing tenants, whether they endured terrible housing conditions, or otherwise. Also, there was no mention regarding those who resided in the Priory of Sion,

Annemasse as well as Mount Sion. The version that was released in CIRCUIT declared that it was the publication of the Federation of French Forces' and was devoted to social as well as philosophical, cultural and research. The first issue was published on July 1. The editor was named in the first issue as Pierre Plantard who was residing at 116 rue Pierre Jouhet in Aulnay, near Bois. Plantard was, naturally the Secretary-General for Sion's Priory of Sion' [66.

In 1973, a book was released that seemed to describe the new issues in CIRCUIT in some depth. The book is titled Les Dessous: D'Une Ambition Politique - New Revelations on the Tresors du Razes et de Gisors"Underground: A Political Ambition New Revelations about the riches of Razes as well as GisorsIt was written by one named 'Mathieu Pauli'. It is, however, a pseudonymous name, and the actual author has not been identified in a definitive way. "Paoli" and his/her agenda will be addressed in the near future. At present, it is sufficient to note the frequency that fake names, false trail are reoccur when trying to research Sion's Priory. Priory of Sion.

According to 'Paoli' she/he inspected a few copies of CIRCUIT within the Versailles Annexe of the Bibliotheque Nationale [National Libraryin Paris]:

The articles cover the occult, grapes, questions of viticulture, magnetics as well as a variety of mysteries and enigmas and also politics. They were written by Pierre Plantard, 'Chyren' (a magus and clairvoyant) and Anne Hisler...and other authors' [7] (Mathieu Paoli).

"Paoli" continued by allegedly invoking some of these articles which are significant because it is believed to "pre-echo" some of the more recent and more bizarre claims made by Sion's Priory of Sion toward the latter half of the 1960s:

* 'In the first issue [of CIRCUIT (1959 Ed)], dedicated to Victor Hugo, the author accumulates allusions, and I quote: "...in that place in 1880, he (Hugo) was the principle column of the Order, the whole world admired this Master who was known so heroically to wear the cross, and whose

sweet perfume of the rose had raised the enthusiasm of the crowd...Victor Hugo died in May 1885...In the midst of national mourning, caravel Paris had lost its Navigator..." The words emphasised in the text reveal the quality of initiate that Victor Hugo was (Rosicrucian Master), and his supreme position within the Order (Nautonnier/Grandmaster) [8] [Pierre Plantard].

Naturally later Sion documents would suggest the fact that Victor Hugo was the Grandmaster of the Priory of Sion, a post that is often known as the Nautonnier. This would appear to be among, perhaps the earliest reference to the particular Sion story that became popular throughout the books Holy Blood, Holy Grail and The Da Vinci Code. But, it must be taken into consideration that the text above is actually a 1973 document that claims to have quoted an article from 1959. We will discuss this in the near future.

Within the multitude of Hermetic articles , there is a distinct political tone which is predicably centered around the'renewal of

France'. One article, purportedly published by someone named 'Adrien sevrette says:

*'When we discuss the issue of family allowances, education as well as construction, in the newest issue of CIRCUIT We say that there is a point with every government, no matter their political beliefs where solutions become more difficult to come up with as the years pass...The solution is only achievable by using new strategies and men, since politics has gone out of fashion. The interesting thing is that we are unable to know this. There is just one thing to consider of economic organization. However, there are still people capable of thinking France like they did during the times of the occupation , when there was no political ambiguity. Patriots were in charge. Resistance fighters did not worry about the political views of their fellow fighters during the war? [9] [attributed to 'Adrien Sévrette"Adrien Sevrette'"Adrien Sevrette"].

The appeal to not pay attention to the political inclinations of "comrades in struggle" is especially interesting. "Sevrette" refers to "the patriots as well as 'the resistance' as separate entities. Does he refer to those who support Vichy's collaborationist regime? Vichy Collaborationist Regime when he refers to patriots, and opponents of the Vichy collaborationist regime when he talks about Resistance fighters? Are he calling attention to the spirit of resistance in wartime in the time that French Communists and Socialists fight together with French Nationalist Fascists and Traditionalists against the Nazis invaders as well as their collaborationist allies?

There are two possible ways to comprehend the above request. First, and the most obvious approach is to interpret it as a "centrist"-style appeal for former enemies to join forces to improve the condition of France. But, the majority of people who believed France required to be renewed were of the opinion that it was precisely the expansion of Socialism that was the issue. In the event that you ask for a dialogue with the Left is then untrue.

It is worth being not forgotten that the patriots were the losers following the fall of Nazi Germany and the French Vichy regime.

Many of the 'patriots were imprisoned and executed due to their ties in the hands of Nazis. In this kind of environment that many were seen as criminals unless they were able to conceal their past involvement with the Nazis. Because of this, it was a duty to the former patriots (to think of the second possible meaning of the word from above) to promote an ideal scenario where people were not worried about the political inclinations of their fellow comrades'. The earlier you start, the better!

His ability to express himself in a manner that makes it hard to definitively state what his motives were, would be a signature of his in the next few years. Although he always seemed to be a member of the militant Rightist camp, he will nonetheless allow enough ambiguity in his writings to be viewed as a possible voice of moderated and even affluent. This would give him a protection against those who say he is an extremist due to his ties to radical Rightist ideas and causes.

Plantard's supporters will, naturally, claim that his ambiguous position was genuine and that he was a Centrist committed to

Rightist causes. However, skeptics may argue that this kind of ambiguity might be an essential element in a time where radical Right was treated as a scourge following the horrendous genocides perpetrated by the Nazis about a decade earlier. Did Plantard's sporadic Centrist "posturing" just an elaborate ploy that was in line with his job in the role of a publicist? It's up to the reader to make the decision. At this point, it is sufficient to point out that, despite his apparent adherence to radical Rightist causes, Plantard's statements were not overwhelmingly extremist, at most in the 1950s.

One aspect worth looking into because it could have important implications as the research moves forward, is the connection to the press releases from Le Monde newspaper attributed to Pierre Plantard in the previous chapter under the pseudonym of 'Captain Way'. It is worth noting that in these press releases, Plantard claimed to be the'secretary of public relations of the Committees of Public Safety that were involved during the right-wing revolution which was able to overthrow the French

Fourth Republic. Plantard mentions a few whom he claimed were his "colleagues" from the Central Committee of Public Safety. Two of them are worth looking into - a journalist known as 'Bonerie-Clarus", and an industrialist known as 'Achille' Fould'.

In the first place, as we have noted in a previous chapter it is very probable that journalist named 'Bonerie-Clarus refers of Camille Bornerie-Clarus. Bornerie-Clarus was a fervent card-carrying Communist in his early days. But, he eventually changed sides and commented in print that the Soviets were paying off Communist elections in France. In 1950, he published the book Mouvement Du Manifeste Aux Francais (The Motion of the Manifesto for the Frenchwhich, as one would expect enough called for an French national revival. According to different sources:

* "Plantard and [a person identified asFould] Fould collaborated together in The Manifesto in support of the French the French, a different'renewal to France movement that was formed after De Gaulle's return the presidency"[10] Lynn Picknett[Lynn Picknett].

As has been demonstrated, that the Movement of the Manifesto to the French appears to be written in the year 1950 by Camille bornerie-Clarus. the man Plantard identified as the chief of the group that had supposedly was to succeed in the role of Central Committee of Public Safety. It is possible that Plantard was in contact with Bornerie-Clarus prior to the return to the power by General de Gaulle? It is possible, at the very least it is possible that Plantard assisted Bornerie-Clarus (along with Monarchist activists Maurice du Parc, a Martin Paris, and A Guibert) to publish the Manifesto in the year 1958.

The only thing that is certain is the fact is that Plantard who, despite his stance as a dedicated Gaullist it is likely that he be a true adherent to the political philosophy that was laid forth in the Manifesto to the French. In issue 4 of the 2nd series of CIRCUIT the 'road map' to the coveted'renewal of France that was released, and was hailed as a "blue-print to be used for the renewal of France:

* Let us hope we can see the 15,000 copies Circuit become a point of contact that is a

beacon of light. We also believe that the patriots' voice can overcome any obstacle, just like in 1940 the time they left France and walked on the doors of the office of the president in Free France. It's the same today and, as we all are French and we are the fighting force with both sides in the quest for the new and healthy France. It is to be built with the same patriotic enthusiasm and with the same determination and a sense of solidarity. That's why we have quoted the phrases of an old philosopher that he proclaimed to us. Each one will recognize the truth of these statements, depending on his own beliefs RESTORATION OF PROVINCES This is the source of the first need to alter the structure of the nation. Departments are an unconstitutional systemthat was developed in the Revolution that was established and defined during the time of the requirements to move (the horses). It is no longer used to reflect anything. The Province is an integral part of France It is the relic of our past; it is the base from which the foundation that is our nationality was created and has its history and customs, as well as its landmarks, often with its own dialect that we love to learn and learn about. The province must be able to establish its own structure for governance and defense inside the framework that is national, and customized to its particular region. We are all aware that the friendly mayors of our municipalities in France do not have any power and are completely dependent on Prefectures...Those who receive their own orders from the government with counter-orders and orders that are soaring in speed and without any accountability [11[CIRCUIT] The "blue-print for renewal" was followed by a host of other political 'needs that claimed to'save France'. The solution offered by the political party distinct from that proposed by de Gaulle, so it is reasonable to conclude that Plantard was, in fact (as previously suggested) an advocate for the Rightist coup that overthrew the Fourth republic , but not a defender for de Gaulle. Plantard's loyalty would appear to have been steadfast to the group that gathered close to Camille Bornerie-Clarus.

In the meantime, before we discuss the person who is referred to as "Achille Fould', it's possible to mention that Bornerie-Clarus ran in the race against Leon Delbecque in late 1958 in a tense political battle. This may indicate that Plantard wasn't a staunch Gaullist despite his position as a member of The Committees of Public Safety. It is also important to note that the race for political power mentioned to above contained Louis Pauwels, the man who wrote the famous Morning of the Magicians, which could be referred to as either for one reason or another"the" French Holy Blood, Holy Grail!

The man mentioned above as 'Achille Fold"is previously mentioned elsewhere, of special attention. Likely, Camille Bornerie Clarus was either misunderstood or mistakenly named by Le Monde as 'Bonerie-Clarus'. Similar to this Gaston Marie Achille-Fould has been mistakenly named "Achille Fould'. There are many fascinating facts concerning Gaston Fould. Fould was an industrialist with a wealth from a renowned and well-known Jewish banker family. The fact that Pierre Plantard had named an "Achille" Fould as a key player in the Committees which had brought de Gaulle back into power, played into the hands of who were a militant Rightist who believed that, and claimed the de Gaulle clan was actually a French traitor who was paid the wages of Jewish bankers!

The claim that the de Gaulle was the puppet of the Judeo-Mason bankers' was previously discussed. Does it seem possible it is possible that the Le Monde press release played an integral role in the laying of this particular charge? Certainly the title employed in the press release by Plantard on his news release, "Achille Fold is evocative of many reasons. The most obvious one is straightforward - for those in aware' the first "Achille Fould was a name that was synonymous with both Jewish banking power and revolutionary. There is some controversy regarding whether Fould was an actual Jew however his family were very rich Jewish bankers.

The first Fould began his life in the year 1800. In 1842, he began his journey into politics as a deputy of an area of the Midi-Pyrenees area, near the Languedoc region that would be important in the subsequent creation of the Priory of Sion mythos. In 1848, a series of revolutions took place across Europe and the world, so many in fact , that the year was dubbed"the Year of Revolutions. It was the very first, and perhaps, the only European decline of the traditional authority. The revolutions extended into South America. At the end, more than fifty nations were hit. The revolutionaries fought for greater democratic participation as well as rights for the workers for the people. These revolutions were, in one in some way or another revolutionary socialist movements, even though the nationalism was a key factor in a variety of. Additionally, Achille Fould is believed to have played a significant role in funding this French versions of the revolutions! Within a year, the revolutions were over. The aristocratic forces as well as the Catholic Church and the army came together and regained control. hundreds of thousands were killed.

In France however the revolt brought about the dissolution of the monarchy that was constitutionally ruled by "King" Louis-Philippe and its replacement through the Second French Republic, led by Louis-Napoleon who was the uncle to Napoleon

Bonaparte. After three years, however, Louis- Napoleon staged an edict of coup and declared himself the Emperor of France and the French Empire. In addition, Achille Fould was a prominent supporter of the coup d'etat, as well as the upcoming revolution. He was the highly powerful French minister of Finance at least four occasions and served as the an advisor for the entire new Imperial Household. To appreciate just the power Fould was, it's worth mentioning his lengthy battle with another influential Jewish financier, James Mayer de Rothschild.

James de Rothschild was the fifth son and the youngest of Mayer Amschel Rothschild, the founder of the mighty Rothschild Jewish banking family. Mayer sent all one of his children to an European capital to establish an institution for banking which was why James was assigned to Paris. His bank venture was so successful that it is believed the sum he earned was 5 times greater than that of Bill Gates! Despite this incredible fortune it was not without a moment in which it appeared James de Rothschild might be destroyed by Achille Fould.

* "The 1830s had passed. The 1840s were declining and the same was the king Louis-Philippe whom Rothschild owned. The popularity of Napoleon was growing and following the former King's departure, Louis-Napoleon was elected President in 1848. Rothschild did not own Napoleon. Achille Fould had. James de Rothschild's rival had loaned the leader money in his voyaging and playboy days. Fould was Napoleon's closest advisor...the president appointed Fould Finance Minister of the Republic"[Italics added[12] [Frederic Moron[Frederic Morton]

The original "Achille Fould was a influential banker from an affluent Jewish family that played an active role in two revolutions as well as an attempted coup d'etat. He was also the one who was believed to have 'owned' King Napoleon III. The fact that another "Achille Fould was so openly associated, as was Pierre Plantard, to the Central Committee of Public Safety that was instrumental in bringing de Gaulle to the presidency after a coup nearly a century after the fact is a remarkable coincidence. In any case, this kind of apparent connection could have sent extremely alarm bells that rang for those who were sure:

* '...de Gaulle was "surrounded by a lot of Jews" He was also told that de Gaulle was the agent of Jewish financiers... and eventhe fact it was said that de Gaulle himself "had Jewish blood" * [italics added] [13Alexander Harrison[Alexander Harrison].

How can this attempt of Pierre Plantard, to associate de Gaulle's return with an 'Achille Fold To be considered?

In the first place, it's worthwhile to highlight how far this is from the worship of goddesses! Furthermore, the "Achille Fould who Plantard was believed to be linked to was in fact Gaston Marie Achille-Fould, who was in reality the great-grandson of the first Achille Fould as the one who owned emperors however, Gaston Marie Achille-Fould was also an influential person on his own. The fact that Plantard was able to claim that he was a conspirator within the pages in Le Monde must surely indicate that Plantard was actually linked to these men. If the claims were not true, Plantard would have been taken care of by such powerful people. He wasn't, which is the complete mockery of researchers, like Jean-Luc Chaumeil who continues to assert that Plantard was just not a fool!

The third reason is that Plantard's association with an 'Achille Fold" goes back nearly 10 years and a half earlier. The details will be discussed in the next section in the Second World War, Plantard and other writers published the magazine Vaincre [Conquerthe World]. The following is a quote from Lynn Picknett:

* 'Achille's Fould had been isolated to be criticized, both as an Jew as well as an Freemason within the issue from January of 1943 in Vaincre. The connection between him and Plantard in 1958 is too to be coincidence which suggests that the publication of wartime and even his [Achille'sdenial of the publication - may have been part of a complex game that was long-term in nature'] [Lynne Pecknett[Lynn Picknett]

However, Picknett doesn't elaborate further or elaborate on the meaning of this game. It is likely that she believes, since Plantard was reportedly 'working alongside' Fould in 1958, Fould must have also been working with Fould in 1943 , when he was dismissed as an Jewish Freemason to Plantard and this implies that they both were involved in a 'work' that was at least 15 years in the creation.

This idea is based on the notion held by some scientists that Pierre Plantard was always simply an 'Gaullist' who was a committed one (meaning that he was a defender of Charles de Gaulle), rather than being the most revered goddess worshipper in the world (a like Dan Brown) or a descendant of Jesus (a like Baigent, Leigh, and Lincoln). According to this particular line of thinking, Plantard was a committed Gaullist in 1958 , when he was the leader of the Central Committee of Public Safety and was an active Gaullist during 1956, when he established the Priory of Sion, which was believed to be the precursor of the Committee as well as an active Gaullist in 1943, when he created Vaincre as an official member of an organization known as"the Alpha Galates. This group, the Alpha Galates and Plantard's association with the group will be discussed in the near course. It is enough for now to mention that some scholars believe that the phrase Alpha Galates translates as 'Primary Gauls' and was intended as a pun meaning 'Number One (followers of de Gaulle'.

If real, would indicate the possibility that Pierre Plantard was part of the French Resistance during the war for the motive it was because de Gaulle was the leader of the French opposition to Nazi rule. This is, in fact what Plantard would later assert. Picknett provides more details, relating on the 1956 CIRCUIT:

* "There's probably more to Circuit than what is apparent It appears that there was. When we looked at the daily articles about increasing damp and purchasing pencils at a wholesale price, something seemed to bother us Something that was a bit familiar. The pattern was beginning to emerge - for instance, the unremorseful selectively removing specific places from the news as well as the publishing of contact details and phone numbers, as well as vague references to political figures... And then it struck us. Circuit was akin to the journals of the time of the Resistance. Every move was watched by the Nazi occupiers as well as their

collaborators in they French liberation fighters were able to conceal the contact information, instructions in code and more beneath a sea of seemingly harmless material, such as regular civic activities. Circuit even claims to be part of a group of local, similar organizations that defend the foyers HLM (Council Housing)and 15.

However, there are people who completely reject this idea and insist that Plantard was an Nazi collaborator and anti-Semite. This skewed view was the source of a very tense disagreement that started as a 'flame-war' online between those who believed that Plantard was"goodie" (a Resistance Hero) and those who claimed Plantard was a "baddie" (an anti-Semitic Nazi collaborator). The difference of opinion among experts on Plantard's history could eventually lead to legal proceedings and possibly imprisonment sentences. This will all be investigated in the near future. In the meantime, it's enough to acknowledge the huge controversy concerning Plantard's wartime activities.

What can be studied in the present is the linkage of the name "Achille Fould"with the return of power to de Gaulle in the year 1958. It is worth noting that the first "Achille Fould" was a highly wealthy Jewish banker who been a supporter of social revolutions as well as an edict that altered history. French history. He had such power that it was believed to be the 'owner' of French King Napoleon III. The fact that Pierre Plantard would associate de Gaulle's return to power as another 'Achille' Fould' is very puzzling because it immediately sparked the most dreadful fears of Rightist French that believe Jewish bankers and Freemasons are behind this latest French coup d'etat and even 'owned' Gaulle. It is crucial to consider the paradoxical nature of this new coup. On one hand nearly all Rightists desired an end to the much-misunderstood Fourth Republic, but on the other hand, many were deeply dissatisfied with de Gaulle.

Naturally, de Gaulle and his supporters have never denied any affiliation in any way with Plantard as well as the Central Committee of Public Safety which is why they are 'Achille's Fould'. According to Baigent, Leigh, and Lincoln observe:

*'We attempted to find additional confirmation and details (linking Plantard with de Gaulle[linking Plantard to de Gaulle]. We looked through all compendia published of de Gaulle's letters notebooks, and notes. It is possible that there was not a mention of Plantard...Neither do any of the Institute Charles de Gaulle - the repository of all archives related to de Gaulle - know of any connections that the General had with a gentleman known as Plantard...When we sought out historians affiliated with the Institute and they considered themselves sceptical...The Director of the Archives at the Institute said that according to their knowledge, they had all of de Gaulle's communications and...the name Plantard was never mentioned in it's 16th (Baigent, Leigh, and Lincoln[16] [Baigent]

In light of these disclaimers of any link with both the General as well as Plantard of the de Gaulle group, Plantard's apparent loyalty to a different political stance and the scathing nature of the press releases issued by Plantard It is evident that Plantard was not a genuine Gaullist in the year 1958. In reality, it can be claimed the fact that

Plantard was a significant enemy of de Gaulle in the year 1958 at least so far as the issue of propaganda was concerned. What does this mean about Plantard's claimed 'Gaullist' credentials between the years 1956 and 1943?

Based on Lynn Picknett, the publishing attack launched by Plantard lead Vaincre on the 'Achille' Fould in 1943 was part of a longer-term plan that involved both men (Plantard and Fould) working together for more than fifteen years. But there's an obvious flaw in this statement. There is a tendency for many writers to make assertions that only appear to be logical when seen in hindsight. It may appear to be logical when seen from the present and the past. However, many historical events must be recognized from the past into the present! The wartime years will be discussed in a subsequent section. It is enough to refer to Picknett's observations as an illustration:

* In Vaincre's January 1943 edition, an article written by the pseudonymous 'Brisieux' targeted one of the Jewish industrialist Achille Fould to be criticized in

both his capacity as an Jew and as a Mason from the Free State. Gaston Marie Achille Fould (1890-1969) was part of a famous Jewish banking family as well as the great-grandson of the famous Achille Fould who was Napoleon I's minister of finance. However, fifteen years later Plantard and Fould would work together in The Manifesto for the French...another "renewal of France movement that was formed after the return of General de Gaulle power in the year 1958. It is unclear what this means however it could suggest that the extent that there is any evidence to suggest that Alpha Galates was pursuing an agenda that was considered to be above the political stances that accompanied the Occupation. What could convince an apparently Jewish banker to work with Plantard who was the editor of the anti-Semitic Vaincre? What is the secret agenda that could be large enough to deflect an individual and even racial affront? [17] [Lynne Picknett[Lynne Picknett

(Before going on in the interest of accuracy, it's important to note the fact that Gaston Achille-Fould was the great-grandson of "the eminent Achille Fould instead of being, as Picknett asserts the grandson of his - Gaston Achille-Fould (1890-1969) son of Charles Achille-Fould (1861-1926) son of Adolphe Fould (1824-1875) the son of Achille Fould (1800-1867)...)

One thing to consider in the above quote written by Lynn Picknett is that most experts believe that 'the pseudonymous "Brisieux"' is probably Pierre Plantard. The second, and perhaps the most important thing to point out that it is crucial to Picknett when it comes to her future claims is concerned to develop the appearance of there is a secret agenda that is large enough to transcend the political sphere that are associated with the Occupation'. To construct this narrative she asks , 'what can convince an unnamed Jewish banker to collaborate with Plantard who was the editor of the seemingly anti-Semitic Vaincre But, this is just a semantic trick that is either accidental or intentional! There is no evidence at present to prove the possibility that Plantard and Fould were in any way involved during the 'Occupation'. Occupation'. In fact, Plantard, or at the very least his newspaper was able to single Fould out for criticism for being both an orthodox Jew as well as a Freemason in a period where doing so could mean total catastrophe for both the person being targeted as well as his or her family!

To put this time in the context of Wikipedia is a great resource:

* "Anti-Semitism was especially virulent during Vichy France during WWII. The Vichy government was openly working in conjunction with Nazi occupiers to determine Jews to be deported and transported to execution camps (about 75,000 of them were killed). In October 1940, despite no demand from the Germans and without any request from the Germans, the Vichy government started implementing anti-Jewish laws (the Statute on Jews) that prohibited their movement in any way, and restricting their access to public areas and professional activities. In 1941 the Vichy government created a General Commissariat to Jewish Affairs (1941-1944) which collaborated with and the Gestapo to begin the process of removing Jews for deportation to concentration camps in

1942... In the period between 1942 until July 1944, more than 76,000 Jews were sent to concentration camps in France and only two hundred survived...It is worth noting that the vast majority of Jews who were deported from France and executed in the Holocaust were not French Jews. Before the severe pressure applied through Nazi Germany, Vichy sought often to safeguard its French-born Jews and especially those who had become part of the French culture or had converted to Catholicism (italics added).

The best method to allow French Jews to survive the Occupation was to maintain their appearance low. When the Vichy government sought to placate the ferocious Nazi anti-Semitism through the deportation of non-French Jews however, the Nazis were intent on the annihilation of all Jews regardless of the nationality. Even though the Vichy government was in no way under control but they were not the only ones to be controlled. Nazis were the true rulers of France. The wealthy French Jews could, and did, utilize their wealth to purchase the way to escape concentration camps, however the situation was incredibly uncertain.

The Nazi perception of Freemasons was just as extreme. Yet again, Wikipedia offers a clear description:

* The Nazis asserted they believed that the highest-degree Masons were willing to be part of the Jewish conspiracy and they claimed that Freemasonry was one of the main reasons Germany lost during in the First World War. The book Mein Kampf, Adolf Hitler declared that Freemasonry has "given in" towards the Jews and is now an excellent instrument to defend their cause and use their'strings to entice the elite of society towards their supposed plans. He added, 'The general pacifist suppression of the national instinct of self-defense that has been triggered by Freemasonry is later propagated to the general population through the press...Consistently thought of as an ideological enemy of Nazism in their public perception, separate parts within the Security Service and later the Reich Security Main Office were created to handle Freemasonry. The prisoners of Freemasonic concentration camps were classified as

'political' prisoners and were required to wear the inverted (point to the left) color red triangle...According to the Nazis the Soviet Union's...inclusion into its participation in League of Nations was engineered by 300'members of Jewish race and the conspirators in Freemasonry'. The 8th of August, 1935 Adolf Hitler announced in the Nazi Party newspaper the final end for all Masonic lodges throughout Germany. The article alleged of a conspiracy between the Fraternity and World Jewry of trying to establish an 'World Republic'. '... In the course of conflict, Freemasonry was banned by an edict for all countries that were either allies to Nazis or under the control of Nazis and/or that were under Nazi control, which included Norway and France...The amount of Freemasons from Nazi nations that were murdered isn't exactly determined, but it's believed that anywhere between the 80,000-200,000 Freemasons were killed under the Nazi regime's.

As you can see the above, it is evident that a powerful and wealthy Jewish Freemason could be viewed in the eyes of those who call themselves the Nazis as their greatest enemy! To have Gaston Achille Fould printed for being both a wealthy Jew as well as an influential Freemason as a result of Pierre Plantard placed the former's life in grave danger. It's hard to think of any plausible scenario to explain this attack during that time frame, apart from simply anti-Semitism. The next question is why was Fould not able to stop being connected to Plantard a few years after?

There are a variety of possibilities which could explain the later connection with Fould as well as Plantard. Fould could have not known about Plantard's wartime connection with Vaincre and could think that 'Brisieux' could be Plantard. Maybe Plantard has been able to heal himself enough that no one could recall his past as a collaborator. According to reports, Plantard always pleaded with his "countrymen" to forgive and forget about his past loyalties (probably which meant forgive and forget about his former collaboration). There were perhaps some men who truly put France first and Fould was among the latter. One of these scenarios could make greater sense that the assertion by Picknett the idea that

Plantard Fould and Fould were working as allies, when Plantard put Fould in such a dire situation in 1943. However, Picknett is certainly to be right in one aspect - it could be more than an accident that "Achille Fould was both publicly 'declared as an Jewish Freemason in 1943 by Plantard in 1943. He was later stated as a Freemason Plantard to be a part in the Central Committee of Public Safety that was allegedly instrumental in bringing back the de Gaulle back to the throne in the year 1958!

It is important to note in this context how frequently the creators of the Priory of Sion mythos use names as an effective background to support the Sion propaganda. In the final sections of this investigation, the use of particular names that convey a certain message will become of major importance. At present, a handful of examples of names will be utilized aside from 'Achille Fold to illustrate the point that these names have been previously studied.

In a prior chapter, it was discovered that of the four foundation members in the Priory of Sion, only Pierre Plantard has been conclusively identified. "Defago" and "Delaval" were not identified in any way. Like we said the phonetic spelling of 'Defago' is like Deffaugt, which is the name given to the French Resistance hero from Annemasse who swore his life for the sake of Jewish children near the end of the conflict. "Delaval" will be studied in the near future. But, before that 'Andre Bonhomme' could be worthy of another consideration.

The first thing to note is that there may be some uncertainty as in relation to "Bonhomme". Absolutely, no photos or videos of 'Bonhomme' have appeared. The date of his birth or long-term address was never disclosed. As we mentioned earlier an investigator from an BBC TV show supposedly spoke on the phone with an individual claiming to be 'Bonhomme in the year 1996. But, it is inquired how exactly did the BBC verify that it was that 'Bonhomme' they spoke to? This research will address the issue. In the meantime, it's worth noting that "Bonhomme" was a term employed by Medieval Christian heretics popularly known as the Cathars, to describe themselves.

"Bonhommes" translates to "Good Men'. If you think about how the Sion narrative would evolve through into the 1960s seemingly "coincidence" is worth mentioning.

"Jean Delaval" was a named in the time that there was a time when the Priory of Sion was registered in 1956. So far as is determined, the name 'Jean Delaval is not known to have been discovered. This, of course, has caused many scholars to conclude that either) the name was a pseudonym that was used by a person who been able to remain unidentified even after more than fifty years of arduous investigation and research, or) the person in question never was ever real and the name was created by Plantard (and possibly Bonhomme) due to reasons of some kind or another.

Whatever the case, the use of the name in question deserves further scrutiny. (Again the reader may be required to acquiesce to the author. Although the information contained in this chapter may seem somewhat flimsy to certain readers, the significance of the decision to use particular names in order to establish subtexts in the Sion narrative will be revealed to be vital as the study develops). One of the most obvious connections that is evident at first is the phonetic connection between 'Jean De Laval' and Jeanne of Laval'. Jeanne de Laval was the spouse of Rene de Anjou (Good King Rene) and the step-mother of Yolande de Bar. The significance here is of course the fact that Rene as well as Yolande were both grandmasters in Sion's Priory of Sion. Rene was believed to have presided over the Priory of Sion from 1418 until 1480 and Yolande was the Priory's Grandmaster from 1480 to 1483. Could this be a mere coincidence? It is now up to the reader think about.

A different interesting connection involves the so-called "Black Madonna". In a previous chapter, different "Black Madonna" have played an important role for Sion's Priory of Sion. In the simplest terms this, they are believed to have played a Black Madonna has played an significant role in the development of the Sion story. It is believed that the Black Madonna in Notre-Dame de Laval was believed to be from the 13th Century and was returned in France from the known Holy Land by King Louis IX ('Saint' Louis) after returning to France from the Crusades.

Conclusion

As was noted throughout this book that the two most extreme opinions that are held by Plantard can also be the ones that are generally accepted by the public. They are: Plantard was either) an ancestor to Jesus and the founder of an ancient, but hidden Goddess practice of worship and 2) an unrepentant fool with fantasies of being a god. However, a thorough analysis of the evidence available is not a convincing support for either of these theories. Instead, Pierre Plantard would clearly seem to be a socially conservative Counter-Revolutionary activist, with perhaps wide ranging contact with other similar men, some of whom may well have been important within that social current. While many French men might be described as socially conservative, not so many could be classed as activists, meaning men who devoted their time and energy to socially conservative and Counter-Revolutionary causes. Plantard was a very busy activist, reportedly putting an enormous amount of time to the advancement of different Rightist goals.

It is certain that the most pressing issue concerns the exact role played by Plantard in the Rightist actions. Was he simply an insignificant underling or was he actually just as important as he was claiming to be? Is the answer in between?

The most important problem is the incredibly puzzling difficult to trace the initial Priory of Sion founding members. If they were really just four men who were worried about their own conditions of living Why is it so difficult despite the massive amount of interestin tracking them in the right direction? Why are they extremely reticent to join their Priory of Sion? The most obvious explanation is the fact that something in this Priory of Sion that they would not like to have. Some scholars argue that the obvious embarrassment was simply a strong refusal to be connected to this Priory of Sion narrative, which would later evolve, initially to become a Merovingian pretender narrative followed by an Jesus Bloodline narrative, and eventually an Goddess narrative. This is how it works:

* "Pierre Plantard and three of his friends created The Priory of Sion for some rather

mundane motive (rising damp, fun and boy-scouting). Due to their conservative social beliefs and beliefs, they registered their organization as an ultra-conservative Catholic lay-order and named the mountain after a nearby one with the added benefit of being a reference towards Jerusalem (Sion) as an important city that played a significant significance in the Christian story. It was the Priory of Sion involved itself in local politics by using as a platform for housing to fight opposition from the Annemasse the political opponents. Things happen until the close of 1956 Sion's Priory of Sion ceased to have any significance. In the beginning of the 1960s, unnoticed by the other three Sion founders, Plantard was able to introduce some of the Priory of Sion name and particulars into a hoax story that he'd created, which he tried to portray his self as the lost Merovingian Pretender of the disbanded French throne. The most comprehensive and widely known explanation of the Plantard "lost Merovingian Pretender" story was published in 1973 in a work by an anonymous author whose name was

"Mathieu Pauli". The author 'Paoli' seemed to have gathered all the various documents including articles, reports, and other sources which had earlier outlined this Merovingian Pretender narrative during the 1960s and then reprinted the story in his publication Undercurrent The Political Ambition: New insights into The Treasures of Gisors and Razes. This book would have a significant role to play in the development of the Jesus bloodline narrative later reconstructed in the works of Baigent, Leigh, and Lincoln in Holy Blood, Holy Grail. Due to the enormous popularity that was Holy Blood, Holy Grail the attention of the world was centered at that particular Priory of Sion and Pierre Plantard. Three of the presumed founding members was shocked to realize that they were connected to a mythical Priory of Sion, and with its fictitious thousand-year old pedigree. Instead of simply denying Plantard's outrageous claims to any interested parties Each of them determined that a complete dissociation was the most sensible option. They were so adept at dissociating themselves, that numerous researchers question whether they actually existed..

This is an conceivable scenario, if one accepts that the other three founders had an almost similar reluctance not to associate in Plantard's Priory of Sion because they were ashamed to be linked with Plantard's later actions. Are there any normalities for three individuals who were supposed to be distinct to behave in this bizarre situation? It is more plausible to suppose that at the very least one of the three would have been publicly and completely transparent regarding the entire affair. Perhaps it is reasonable to believe that at the very least one of the three could have sought out the inevitable media attention that came with after the release of Holy Blood, Holy Grail at least to forcefully to denounce Plantard and his assertions as absurd. It is possible that the men were interrogated. But, Chaumeil claimed to have located these men and conducted an interview with them in an era when he didn't even know their names! Only the claimed Bonhomme interviews have any chance of being legitimate and, as pointed out there are serious problems regarding those interviews as well.

However, the main problem with this idea is that it doesn't make sense of the supposed claim of the Priory of Sion was non-political. The reader must remember how the mayor of Annemasse was clear to it was a political pressure group. Priory of Sion is an organization for political pressure, Plantard was a representative of the political system and Priory literature was distinctly political. The title of 'Mathieu's book' about Sion's Priory of Sion was Undercurrent An Ambition for Politics! It is clear that Paoli believed his book about the Priory of Sion was specifically politically motivated. It seems reasonable to suppose that the letter of Andre Bonhomme from 1976 in which he announced his resignation as director of the Priory of Sion was in reaction to the publication and response to the claims in Undercurrent An Ambition Political. Ambition.

However, this doesn't seem to contradict the earlier scenario. It does possibly confirm the idea of Pierre Plantard 'resurrected' the Priory of Sion name without being aware of his fellows as well. When this'resurrection was revealed after it was revealed in Undercurrent The Political Ambition Bonhomme swiftly moved to disengage himself. The fact that all of this does not clarify why each was so determined to disengage their respective sides away from their respective Priory of Sion. Why these men should be embarrassed by the seemingly innocent connection with an individual who was later to make wildly exaggerated claims about his own significance is difficult to comprehend. It's also extremely difficult to grasp why Andre Bonhomme was determined to proclaim his Priory of Sion non-political, and also so anxious to make any broad comment about any aspect of the Priory of Sion at all. All evidence available apart from this questionable assertion, seems to indicate the reverse direction, namely in that Priory of Sion was specifically politically-motivated!

If that's true, then it would surely explain the reason why one of the Priory of Sion founders wished to remain anonymous. The 1950s France had been caught in the midst of a turbulent period of political turmoil. Some felt that Counter-Revolutionary activism was a very real necessity if the spread of Liberalism, Secularism, and Socialism was to be halted. Numerous groups were created in this direction at the time. But, 20 years later what was considered acceptable a few years earlier was now considered to be a fashion faux pas in the wake of opinions about race nationalists, gender, and so on had changed. Many people were no longer willing being associated with extremist political views particularly if their earlier actions were seditious as well as criminal. In addition numerous Rightists who had backed de Gaulle in the past would later hesitate to admit they did so given the way he failed to "save" French Algeria.

The second scenario is similar to this:

* A small number of men that were united by their traditional Christian convictions and activism created the Traditionalist Catholic order of laymen. They believed that this lay-order could be a factor in the'renewal' that was being attempted in France and the world. This was a'renewal which was

promoted by a variety of Rightist social commentators such as Paul Le Cour and Jean Ousset. The'renewal' was an end to the 'traditional' values and social hierarchy. It was the Priory of Sion used the local housing situation to propel their own, as well as Pierre Plantard, into local political affairs. The events took their course then Pierre Plantard moved on to Paris. Within a year and a half of establishing, or perhaps re-establishing his credentials as a Counter-Revolutionary political activist, Plantard was presenting himself as the spokesman for the Central Committee of Public Safety during the Rightist coup that placed Charles de Gaulle on the French 'throne''.

Plantard claimed to be a journalist at the time. It is very likely that his 'work' for the CIRCUIT "magazine" was the only "journalism" that he actually did. It was demonstrated earlier that it is highly unlikely that Plantard would have made his Central Committee Spokesman claim without having played a role in the plot to end the Fourth Republic. It seems reasonable to believe that his role in Annemasse was a factor in his appearance one day after, in a key section of the Committees of Public Safety. The reader will recall that Abraham Karlikow described the first French based Committees of Public Safety as pre-existing, non-Gaullist, Counter-Revolutionary groupings, which then tried to insert themselves into the evolving political process by use of clever propaganda. One of the principal designers of this clever application in propaganda was Pierre Plantard.

Lightning Source UK Ltd.
Milton Keynes UK
UKHW021941090223
416794UK00018B/203